Loyalty and Rewards
Complete Self-Assessment Guide

The guidance in this Self-Assessment is based on Loyalty and ... best practices and standards in business process architecture, design and quality management. The guidance is also based on the professional judgment of the individual collaborators listed in the Acknowledgments.

Table of Contents

About The Art of Service

The Art of Service, Business Process Architects since 2000, is dedicated to helping stakeholders achieve excellence.

Defining, designing, creating, and implementing a process to solve a stakeholders challenge or meet an objective is the most valuable role… In EVERY group, company, organization and department.

Unless you're talking a one-time, single-use project, there should be a process. Whether that process is managed and implemented by humans, AI, or a combination of the two, it needs to be designed by someone with a complex enough perspective to ask the right questions.

Someone capable of asking the right questions and step back and say, 'What are we really trying to accomplish here? And is there a different way to look at it?'

With The Art of Service's Standard Requirements Self-Assessments, we empower people who can do just that — whether their title is marketer, entrepreneur, manager, salesperson, consultant, Business Process Manager, executive assistant, IT Manager, CIO etc... —they are the people who rule the future. They are people who watch the process as it happens, and ask the right questions to make the process work better.

Contact us when you need any support with this Self-Assessment and any help with templates, blue-prints and examples of standard documents you might need:

http://theartofservice.com
service@theartofservice.com

Acknowledgments

This checklist was developed under the auspices of The Art of Service, chaired by Gerardus Blokdyk.

Representatives from several client companies participated in the preparation of this Self-Assessment.

Our deepest gratitude goes out to Matt Champagne, Ph.D. Surveys Expert, for his invaluable help and advise in structuring the Self Assessment.

In addition, we are thankful for the design and printing services provided.

Included Resources - how to access

Included with your purchase of the book is the Loyalty and Rewards Self-Assessment Spreadsheet Dashboard which contains all questions and Self-Assessment areas and auto-generates insights, graphs, and project RACI planning - all with examples to get you started right away.

How? Simply send an email to
access@theartofservice.com
with this books' title in the subject to get the Loyalty and Rewards Self Assessment Tool right away.

You will receive the following contents with New and Updated specific criteria:
- The latest quick edition of the book in PDF
- The latest complete edition of the book in PDF, which criteria correspond to the criteria in...
- The Self-Assessment Excel Dashboard, and...
- Example pre-filled Self-Assessment Excel Dashboard to get familiar with results generation
- ...plus an extra, special, resource that helps you with project managing.

INCLUDES LIFETIME SELF ASSESSMENT UPDATES

Every self assessment comes with Lifetime Updates and Lifetime Free Updated Books. Lifetime Updates is an industry-first feature which allows you to receive verified self assessment updates, ensuring you always have the most accurate information at your fingertips.

Get it now- you will be glad you did - do it now, before you forget.

Send an email to **access@theartofservice.com** with this books' title in the subject to get the Loyalty and Rewards Self Assessment Tool right away.

Your feedback is invaluable to us

If you recently bought this book, we would love to hear from you! You can do this by writing a review on amazon (or the online store where you purchased this book) about your last purchase! As part of our continual service improvement process, we love to hear real client experiences and feedback.

How does it work?
To post a review on Amazon, just log in to your account and click on the Create Your Own Review button (under Customer Reviews) of the relevant product page. You can find examples of product reviews in Amazon. If you purchased from another online store, simply follow their procedures.

What happens when I submit my review?
Once you have submitted your review, send us an email at review@theartofservice.com with the link to your review so we can properly thank you for your feedback.

Purpose of this Self-Assessment

This Self-Assessment has been developed to improve understanding of the requirements and elements of Loyalty and Rewards, based on best practices and standards in business process architecture, design and quality management.

It is designed to allow for a rapid Self-Assessment to determine how closely existing management practices and procedures correspond to the elements of the Self-Assessment.

The criteria of requirements and elements of Loyalty and Rewards have been rephrased in the format of a Self-Assessment questionnaire, with a seven-criterion scoring system, as explained in this document.

In this format, even with limited background knowledge of

Loyalty and Rewards, a manager can quickly review existing operations to determine how they measure up to the standards. This in turn can serve as the starting point of a 'gap analysis' to identify management tools or system elements that might usefully be implemented in the organization to help improve overall performance.

How to use the Self-Assessment

On the following pages are a series of questions to identify to what extent your Loyalty and Rewards initiative is complete in comparison to the requirements set in standards.

To facilitate answering the questions, there is a space in front of each question to enter a score on a scale of '1' to '5'.

1 Strongly Disagree

2 Disagree

3 Neutral

4 Agree

5 Strongly Agree

Read the question and rate it with the following in front of mind:

**'In my belief,
the answer to this question is clearly defined'.**

There are two ways in which you can choose to interpret this statement;
1. how aware are you that the answer to the question is clearly defined
2. for more in-depth analysis you can choose to gather

evidence and confirm the answer to the question. This obviously will take more time, most Self-Assessment users opt for the first way to interpret the question and dig deeper later on based on the outcome of the overall Self-Assessment.

A score of '1' would mean that the answer is not clear at all, where a '5' would mean the answer is crystal clear and defined. Leave emtpy when the question is not applicable or you don't want to answer it, you can skip it without affecting your score. Write your score in the space provided.

After you have responded to all the appropriate statements in each section, compute your average score for that section, using the formula provided, and round to the nearest tenth. Then transfer to the corresponding spoke in the Loyalty and Rewards Scorecard on the second next page of the Self-Assessment.

Your completed Loyalty and Rewards Scorecard will give you a clear presentation of which Loyalty and Rewards areas need attention.

Loyalty and Rewards
Scorecard Example

Example of how the finalized Scorecard can look like:

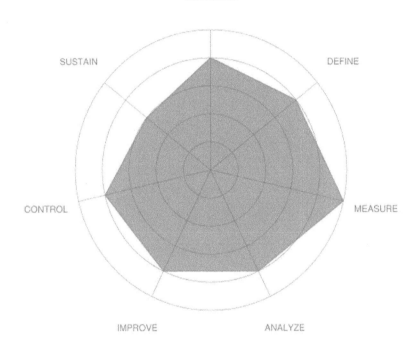

Loyalty and Rewards Scorecard

Your Scores:

BEGINNING OF THE SELF-ASSESSMENT:

CRITERION #1: RECOGNIZE

INTENT: Be aware of the need for change. Recognize that there is an unfavorable variation, problem or symptom.

In my belief, the answer to this question is clearly defined:

5 Strongly Agree

4 Agree

3 Neutral

2 Disagree

1 Strongly Disagree

1. Who had the original idea?
<--- Score

2. When a Loyalty and Rewards manager recognizes a problem, what options are available?
<--- Score

3. What problems are you facing and how do you consider Loyalty and Rewards will circumvent those

obstacles?
<--- Score

4. What does Loyalty and Rewards success mean to the stakeholders?
<--- Score

5. What else needs to be measured?
<--- Score

6. What do you need to start doing?
<--- Score

7. How does it fit into your organizational needs and tasks?
<--- Score

8. Will it solve real problems?
<--- Score

9. Does Loyalty and Rewards create potential expectations in other areas that need to be recognized and considered?
<--- Score

10. Will a response program recognize when a crisis occurs and provide some level of response?
<--- Score

11. What situation(s) led to this Loyalty and Rewards Self Assessment?
<--- Score

12. For your Loyalty and Rewards project, identify and describe the business environment, is there more than one layer to the business environment?

<--- Score

13. Will Loyalty and Rewards deliverables need to be tested and, if so, by whom?
<--- Score

14. What should be considered when identifying available resources, constraints, and deadlines?
<--- Score

15. Who needs to know about Loyalty and Rewards?
<--- Score

16. Are controls defined to recognize and contain problems?
<--- Score

17. What training and capacity building actions are needed to implement proposed reforms?
<--- Score

18. Think about the people you identified for your Loyalty and Rewards project and the project responsibilities you would assign to them. what kind of training do you think they would need to perform these responsibilities effectively?
<--- Score

19. How much are sponsors, customers, partners, stakeholders involved in Loyalty and Rewards? In other words, what are the risks, if Loyalty and Rewards does not deliver successfully?
<--- Score

20. Who defines the rules in relation to any given issue?

<--- Score

21. How are the Loyalty and Rewards's objectives aligned to the organization's overall business strategy?
<--- Score

22. Have you identified your Loyalty and Rewards key performance indicators?
<--- Score

23. Are there recognized Loyalty and Rewards problems?
<--- Score

24. How are you going to measure success?
<--- Score

25. Are there any specific expectations or concerns about the Loyalty and Rewards team, Loyalty and Rewards itself?
<--- Score

26. What prevents you from making the changes you know will make you a more effective Loyalty and Rewards leader?
<--- Score

27. Do you know what you need to know about Loyalty and Rewards?
<--- Score

28. What are the business objectives to be achieved with Loyalty and Rewards?
<--- Score

29. Who else hopes to benefit from it?
<--- Score

30. Is it clear when you think of the day ahead of you what activities and tasks you need to complete?
<--- Score

31. Consider your own Loyalty and Rewards project, what types of organizational problems do you think might be causing or affecting your problem, based on the work done so far?
<--- Score

32. Will new equipment/products be required to facilitate Loyalty and Rewards delivery, for example is new software needed?
<--- Score

33. What tools and technologies are needed for a custom Loyalty and Rewards project?
<--- Score

34. How do you assess your Loyalty and Rewards workforce capability and capacity needs, including skills, competencies, and staffing levels?
<--- Score

35. How can auditing be a preventative security measure?
<--- Score

36. What are your needs in relation to Loyalty and Rewards skills, labor, equipment, and markets?
<--- Score

37. As a sponsor, customer or management, how

important is it to meet goals, objectives?
<--- Score

38. Does your organization need more Loyalty and
Rewards education?
<--- Score

39. What vendors make products that address the
Loyalty and Rewards needs?
<--- Score

40. What are the expected benefits of Loyalty and
Rewards to the business?
<--- Score

41. How do you take a forward-looking perspective in
identifying Loyalty and Rewards research related to
market response and models?
<--- Score

42. What would happen if Loyalty and Rewards
weren't done?
<--- Score

43. Can management personnel recognize the
monetary benefit of Loyalty and Rewards?
<--- Score

44. What is the smallest subset of the problem you
can usefully solve?
<--- Score

45. Are there Loyalty and Rewards problems defined?
<--- Score

46. How do you identify the kinds of information that

you will need?
<--- Score

47. What information do users need?
<--- Score

Add up total points for this section:
_ _ _ _ _ = Total points for this section

Divided by: _ _ _ _ _ _ (number of
statements answered) = _ _ _ _ _ _
Average score for this section

Transfer your score to the Loyalty and
Rewards Index at the beginning of the
Self-Assessment.

CRITERION #2: DEFINE:

INTENT: Formulate the business problem. Define the problem, needs and objectives.

In my belief, the answer to this question is clearly defined:

5 Strongly Agree

4 Agree

3 Neutral

2 Disagree

1 Strongly Disagree

1. Is Loyalty and Rewards linked to key business goals and objectives?
<--- Score

2. Do you all define Loyalty and Rewards in the same way?
<--- Score

3. Are improvement team members fully trained on

Loyalty and Rewards?
<--- Score

4. Is data collected and displayed to better understand customer(s) critical needs and requirements.
<--- Score

5. What are the Roles and Responsibilities for each team member and its leadership? Where is this documented?
<--- Score

6. What specifically is the problem? Where does it occur? When does it occur? What is its extent?
<--- Score

7. Has a high-level 'as is' process map been completed, verified and validated?
<--- Score

8. What would be the goal or target for a Loyalty and Rewards's improvement team?
<--- Score

9. Have all basic functions of Loyalty and Rewards been defined?
<--- Score

10. Is there a critical path to deliver Loyalty and Rewards results?
<--- Score

11. Has the direction changed at all during the course of Loyalty and Rewards? If so, when did it change and why?
<--- Score

12. Is a fully trained team formed, supported, and committed to work on the Loyalty and Rewards improvements?
<--- Score

13. Will team members perform Loyalty and Rewards work when assigned and in a timely fashion?
<--- Score

14. What critical content must be communicated – who, what, when, where, and how?
<--- Score

15. Are there any constraints known that bear on the ability to perform Loyalty and Rewards work? How is the team addressing them?
<--- Score

16. Are roles and responsibilities formally defined?
<--- Score

17. Is there a Loyalty and Rewards management charter, including business case, problem and goal statements, scope, milestones, roles and responsibilities, communication plan?
<--- Score

18. Are customer(s) identified and segmented according to their different needs and requirements?
<--- Score

19. Has/have the customer(s) been identified?
<--- Score

20. In what way can you redefine the criteria of choice

clients have in your category in your favor?
<--- Score

21. Is the team adequately staffed with the desired cross-functionality? If not, what additional resources are available to the team?
<--- Score

22. In what way can you redefine the criteria of choice in your category in your favor?
<--- Score

23. Is there regularly 100% attendance at the team meetings? If not, have appointed substitutes attended to preserve cross-functionality and full representation?
<--- Score

24. Is the Loyalty and Rewards scope manageable?
<--- Score

25. Are team charters developed?
<--- Score

26. Is the scope of Loyalty and Rewards defined?
<--- Score

27. If substitutes have been appointed, have they been briefed on the Loyalty and Rewards goals and received regular communications as to the progress to date?
<--- Score

28. How did the Loyalty and Rewards manager receive input to the development of a Loyalty and Rewards improvement plan and the estimated completion

dates/times of each activity?
<--- Score

29. Does the team have regular meetings?
<--- Score

30. What are the record-keeping requirements of Loyalty and Rewards activities?
<--- Score

31. Are there different segments of customers?
<--- Score

32. Will team members regularly document their Loyalty and Rewards work?
<--- Score

33. Is it clearly defined in and to your organization what you do?
<--- Score

34. Have specific policy objectives been defined?
<--- Score

35. When was the Loyalty and Rewards start date?
<--- Score

36. Are different versions of process maps needed to account for the different types of inputs?
<--- Score

37. Has the Loyalty and Rewards work been fairly and/or equitably divided and delegated among team members who are qualified and capable to perform the work? Has everyone contributed?
<--- Score

38. What are the rough order estimates on cost savings/opportunities that Loyalty and Rewards brings?
<--- Score

39. What defines best in class?
<--- Score

40. Are business processes mapped?
<--- Score

41. How will variation in the actual durations of each activity be dealt with to ensure that the expected Loyalty and Rewards results are met?
<--- Score

42. Have the customer needs been translated into specific, measurable requirements? How?
<--- Score

43. Has a project plan, Gantt chart, or similar been developed/completed?
<--- Score

44. Are audit criteria, scope, frequency and methods defined?
<--- Score

45. What baselines are required to be defined and managed?
<--- Score

46. Is Loyalty and Rewards currently on schedule according to the plan?
<--- Score

47. Is there a completed SIPOC representation, describing the Suppliers, Inputs, Process, Outputs, and Customers?
<--- Score

48. Are approval levels defined for contracts and supplements to contracts?
<--- Score

49. Is full participation by members in regularly held team meetings guaranteed?
<--- Score

50. Is the current 'as is' process being followed? If not, what are the discrepancies?
<--- Score

51. Is the team sponsored by a champion or business leader?
<--- Score

52. Do the problem and goal statements meet the SMART criteria (specific, measurable, attainable, relevant, and time-bound)?
<--- Score

53. Have all of the relationships been defined properly?
<--- Score

54. Are required metrics defined, what are they?
<--- Score

55. How often are the team meetings?
<--- Score

56. Are task requirements clearly defined?
<--- Score

57. What are the boundaries of the scope? What is in bounds and what is not? What is the start point? What is the stop point?
<--- Score

58. What constraints exist that might impact the team?
<--- Score

59. Has anyone else (internal or external to the organization) attempted to solve this problem or a similar one before? If so, what knowledge can be leveraged from these previous efforts?
<--- Score

60. How would you define the culture at your organization, how susceptible is it to Loyalty and Rewards changes?
<--- Score

61. How will the Loyalty and Rewards team and the organization measure complete success of Loyalty and Rewards?
<--- Score

62. Is the team equipped with available and reliable resources?
<--- Score

63. When are meeting minutes sent out? Who is on the distribution list?
<--- Score

64. Has everyone on the team, including the team leaders, been properly trained?
<--- Score

65. What customer feedback methods were used to solicit their input?
<--- Score

66. How does the Loyalty and Rewards manager ensure against scope creep?
<--- Score

67. When is the estimated completion date?
<--- Score

68. How is the team tracking and documenting its work?
<--- Score

69. How would you define Loyalty and Rewards leadership?
<--- Score

70. Is the improvement team aware of the different versions of a process: what they think it is vs. what it actually is vs. what it should be vs. what it could be?
<--- Score

71. Is the team formed and are team leaders (Coaches and Management Leads) assigned?
<--- Score

72. Has a team charter been developed and communicated?
<--- Score

73. Is Loyalty and Rewards required?
<--- Score

74. How and when will the baselines be defined?
<--- Score

75. Who defines (or who defined) the rules and roles?
<--- Score

76. What key business process output measure(s) does Loyalty and Rewards leverage and how?
<--- Score

77. How was the 'as is' process map developed, reviewed, verified and validated?
<--- Score

78. What are the compelling business reasons for embarking on Loyalty and Rewards?
<--- Score

79. Is there a completed, verified, and validated high-level 'as is' (not 'should be' or 'could be') business process map?
<--- Score

80. Are customers identified and high impact areas defined?
<--- Score

81. How can the value of Loyalty and Rewards be defined?
<--- Score

82. Who are the Loyalty and Rewards improvement

team members, including Management Leads and Coaches?
<--- Score

83. Has the improvement team collected the 'voice of the customer' (obtained feedback – qualitative and quantitative)?
<--- Score

84. How do you keep key subject matter experts in the loop?
<--- Score

85. What are the dynamics of the communication plan?
<--- Score

86. Are accountability and ownership for Loyalty and Rewards clearly defined?
<--- Score

Add up total points for this section:
_ _ _ _ _ = Total points for this section

Divided by: _ _ _ _ _ _ (number of statements answered) = _ _ _ _ _ _
Average score for this section

Transfer your score to the Loyalty and Rewards Index at the beginning of the Self-Assessment.

CRITERION #3: MEASURE:

INTENT: Gather the correct data.
Measure the current performance and
evolution of the situation.

In my belief, the answer to this
question is clearly defined:

5 Strongly Agree

4 Agree

3 Neutral

2 Disagree

1 Strongly Disagree

1. How do you know that any Loyalty and Rewards
analysis is complete and comprehensive?
<--- Score

2. What is an unallowable cost?
<--- Score

3. How is performance measured?
<--- Score

4. Have changes been properly/adequately analyzed for effect?
<--- Score

5. Have all non-recommended alternatives been analyzed in sufficient detail?
<--- Score

6. How do you do risk analysis of rare, cascading, catastrophic events?
<--- Score

7. How is progress measured?
<--- Score

8. Which measures and indicators matter?
<--- Score

9. How will measures be used to manage and adapt?
<--- Score

10. How do your measurements capture actionable Loyalty and Rewards information for use in exceeding your customers expectations and securing your customers engagement?
<--- Score

11. How frequently do you track measures?
<--- Score

12. What is measured? Why?
<--- Score

13. How frequently do you track Loyalty and Rewards measures?

<--- Score

14. How do you identify and analyze stakeholders and their interests?
<--- Score

15. Was a data collection plan established?
<--- Score

16. What are the costs of reform?
<--- Score

17. Do you aggressively reward and promote the people who have the biggest impact on creating excellent Loyalty and Rewards services/products?
<--- Score

18. What potential environmental factors impact the Loyalty and Rewards effort?
<--- Score

19. How do you control the overall costs of your work processes?
<--- Score

20. Does Loyalty and Rewards analysis isolate the fundamental causes of problems?
<--- Score

21. Have you found any 'ground fruit' or 'low-hanging fruit' for immediate remedies to the gap in performance?
<--- Score

22. What particular quality tools did the team find helpful in establishing measurements?

<--- Score

23. Are key measures identified and agreed upon?
<--- Score

24. What is the right balance of time and resources between investigation, analysis, and discussion and dissemination?
<--- Score

25. How do you measure success?
<--- Score

26. What are your key Loyalty and Rewards indicators that you will measure, analyze and track?
<--- Score

27. How will success or failure be measured?
<--- Score

28. How do you focus on what is right -not who is right?
<--- Score

29. Are losses documented, analyzed, and remedial processes developed to prevent future losses?
<--- Score

30. What do you measure and why?
<--- Score

31. How do you measure lifecycle phases?
<--- Score

32. Do staff have the necessary skills to collect, analyze, and report data?

<--- Score

33. Have the concerns of stakeholders to help identify and define potential barriers been obtained and analyzed?
<--- Score

34. Is it possible to estimate the impact of unanticipated complexity such as wrong or failed assumptions, feedback, etc. on proposed reforms?
<--- Score

35. Among the Loyalty and Rewards product and service cost to be estimated, which is considered hardest to estimate?
<--- Score

36. Is data collected on key measures that were identified?
<--- Score

37. Does your organization systematically track and analyze outcomes related for accountability and quality improvement?
<--- Score

38. How to measure variability?
<--- Score

39. How is the value delivered by Loyalty and Rewards being measured?
<--- Score

40. What is the total cost related to deploying Loyalty and Rewards, including any consulting or professional services?

<--- Score

41. Are there any easy-to-implement alternatives to Loyalty and Rewards? Sometimes other solutions are available that do not require the cost implications of a full-blown project?
<--- Score

42. What methods are feasible and acceptable to estimate the impact of reforms?
<--- Score

43. How will you measure your Loyalty and Rewards effectiveness?
<--- Score

44. Are process variation components displayed/ communicated using suitable charts, graphs, plots?
<--- Score

45. What data was collected (past, present, future/ ongoing)?
<--- Score

46. What has the team done to assure the stability and accuracy of the measurement process?
<--- Score

47. What charts has the team used to display the components of variation in the process?
<--- Score

48. Does Loyalty and Rewards systematically track and analyze outcomes for accountability and quality improvement?
<--- Score

49. How are you going to measure success?
<--- Score

50. What are your customers expectations and measures?
<--- Score

51. Are there measurements based on task performance?
<--- Score

52. Have the types of risks that may impact Loyalty and Rewards been identified and analyzed?
<--- Score

53. Is a solid data collection plan established that includes measurement systems analysis?
<--- Score

54. Are missed Loyalty and Rewards opportunities costing your organization money?
<--- Score

55. The approach of traditional Loyalty and Rewards works for detail complexity but is focused on a systematic approach rather than an understanding of the nature of systems themselves, what approach will permit your organization to deal with the kind of unpredictable emergent behaviors that dynamic complexity can introduce?
<--- Score

56. Will Loyalty and Rewards have an impact on current business continuity, disaster recovery processes and/or infrastructure?

<--- Score

57. Why do the measurements/indicators matter?
<--- Score

58. Why do you expend time and effort to implement measurement, for whom?
<--- Score

59. Is the solution cost-effective?
<--- Score

60. Is data collection planned and executed?
<--- Score

61. Are the measurements objective?
<--- Score

62. Are you taking your company in the direction of better and revenue or cheaper and cost?
<--- Score

63. What are the agreed upon definitions of the high impact areas, defect(s), unit(s), and opportunities that will figure into the process capability metrics?
<--- Score

64. Who participated in the data collection for measurements?
<--- Score

65. Can you do Loyalty and Rewards without complex (expensive) analysis?
<--- Score

66. How will effects be measured?

<--- Score

67. Are the units of measure consistent?
<--- Score

68. Who should receive measurement reports?
<--- Score

69. How do you aggregate measures across priorities?
<--- Score

70. What are the types and number of measures to use?
<--- Score

71. Does the Loyalty and Rewards task fit the client's priorities?
<--- Score

72. What measurements are possible, practicable and meaningful?
<--- Score

73. Is long term and short term variability accounted for?
<--- Score

74. What evidence is there and what is measured?
<--- Score

75. Is Process Variation Displayed/Communicated?
<--- Score

76. Is there a Performance Baseline?
<--- Score

77. What are your key Loyalty and Rewards organizational performance measures, including key short and longer-term financial measures?
<--- Score

78. Where is it measured?
<--- Score

79. How do you stay flexible and focused to recognize larger Loyalty and Rewards results?
<--- Score

80. What are the key input variables? What are the key process variables? What are the key output variables?
<--- Score

81. Is key measure data collection planned and executed, process variation displayed and communicated and performance baselined?
<--- Score

82. Are high impact defects defined and identified in the business process?
<--- Score

83. Do you effectively measure and reward individual and team performance?
<--- Score

84. What are the uncertainties surrounding estimates of impact?
<--- Score

85. Can you measure the return on analysis?
<--- Score

86. What relevant entities could be measured?
<--- Score

87. How can you measure Loyalty and Rewards in a systematic way?
<--- Score

88. What key measures identified indicate the performance of the business process?
<--- Score

89. Which stakeholder characteristics are analyzed?
<--- Score

90. How will your organization measure success?
<--- Score

91. How are measurements made?
<--- Score

92. How will you measure success?
<--- Score

93. What measurements are being captured?
<--- Score

94. Does Loyalty and Rewards analysis show the relationships among important Loyalty and Rewards factors?
<--- Score

95. How large is the gap between current performance and the customer-specified (goal) performance?
<--- Score

96. How can you measure the performance?
<--- Score

Add up total points for this section:
_ _ _ _ _ = Total points for this section

Divided by: _ _ _ _ _ _ (number of
statements answered) = _ _ _ _ _ _
Average score for this section

Transfer your score to the Loyalty and
Rewards Index at the beginning of the
Self-Assessment.

CRITERION #4: ANALYZE:

INTENT: Analyze causes, assumptions and hypotheses.

In my belief, the answer to this question is clearly defined:

5 Strongly Agree

4 Agree

3 Neutral

2 Disagree

1 Strongly Disagree

1. Think about some of the processes you undertake within your organization, which do you own?
<--- Score

2. Is the performance gap determined?
<--- Score

3. What are your current levels and trends in key measures or indicators of Loyalty and Rewards product and process performance that are important

to and directly serve your customers? How do these results compare with the performance of your competitors and other organizations with similar offerings?
<--- Score

4. What controls do you have in place to protect data?
<--- Score

5. How do you implement and manage your work processes to ensure that they meet design requirements?
<--- Score

6. What tools were used to generate the list of possible causes?
<--- Score

7. What were the financial benefits resulting from any 'ground fruit or low-hanging fruit' (quick fixes)?
<--- Score

8. A compounding model resolution with available relevant data can often provide insight towards a solution methodology; which Loyalty and Rewards models, tools and techniques are necessary?
<--- Score

9. Were Pareto charts (or similar) used to portray the 'heavy hitters' (or key sources of variation)?
<--- Score

10. What are the disruptive Loyalty and Rewards technologies that enable your organization to radically change your business processes?
<--- Score

11. Is Data and process analysis, root cause analysis and quantifying the gap/opportunity in place?
<--- Score

12. Was a cause-and-effect diagram used to explore the different types of causes (or sources of variation)?
<--- Score

13. What successful thing are you doing today that may be blinding you to new growth opportunities?
<--- Score

14. How often will data be collected for measures?
<--- Score

15. How do you use Loyalty and Rewards data and information to support organizational decision making and innovation?
<--- Score

16. Have any additional benefits been identified that will result from closing all or most of the gaps?
<--- Score

17. Is the Loyalty and Rewards process severely broken such that a re-design is necessary?
<--- Score

18. How do you measure the operational performance of your key work systems and processes, including productivity, cycle time, and other appropriate measures of process effectiveness, efficiency, and innovation?
<--- Score

19. Were any designed experiments used to generate additional insight into the data analysis?
<--- Score

20. What are the best opportunities for value improvement?
<--- Score

21. What other organizational variables, such as reward systems or communication systems, affect the performance of this Loyalty and Rewards process?
<--- Score

22. What tools were used to narrow the list of possible causes?
<--- Score

23. Can you add value to the current Loyalty and Rewards decision-making process (largely qualitative) by incorporating uncertainty modeling (more quantitative)?
<--- Score

24. What does the data say about the performance of the business process?
<--- Score

25. What quality tools were used to get through the analyze phase?
<--- Score

26. How was the detailed process map generated, verified, and validated?
<--- Score

27. What were the crucial 'moments of truth' on the

process map?
<--- Score

28. Where is the data coming from to measure compliance?
<--- Score

29. What process should you select for improvement?
<--- Score

30. Were there any improvement opportunities identified from the process analysis?
<--- Score

31. Do several people in different organizational units assist with the Loyalty and Rewards process?
<--- Score

32. How do your work systems and key work processes relate to and capitalize on your core competencies?
<--- Score

33. Have the problem and goal statements been updated to reflect the additional knowledge gained from the analyze phase?
<--- Score

34. Think about the functions involved in your Loyalty and Rewards project, what processes flow from these functions?
<--- Score

35. An organizationally feasible system request is one that considers the mission, goals and objectives of the organization. Key questions are: is the Loyalty and

Rewards solution request practical and will it solve a problem or take advantage of an opportunity to achieve company goals?

<--- Score

36. What is the cost of poor quality as supported by the team's analysis?

<--- Score

37. Are gaps between current performance and the goal performance identified?

<--- Score

38. How do you promote understanding that opportunity for improvement is not criticism of the status quo, or the people who created the status quo?

<--- Score

39. Did any value-added analysis or 'lean thinking' take place to identify some of the gaps shown on the 'as is' process map?

<--- Score

40. When conducting a business process reengineering study, what do you look for when trying to identify business processes to change?

<--- Score

41. What are your best practices for minimizing Loyalty and Rewards project risk, while demonstrating incremental value and quick wins throughout the Loyalty and Rewards project lifecycle?

<--- Score

42. Do your leaders quickly bounce back from setbacks?

<--- Score

43. Identify an operational issue in your organization. for example, could a particular task be done more quickly or more efficiently by Loyalty and Rewards?
<--- Score

44. How does the organization define, manage, and improve its Loyalty and Rewards processes?
<--- Score

45. Record-keeping requirements flow from the records needed as inputs, outputs, controls and for transformation of a Loyalty and Rewards process. Are the records needed as inputs to the Loyalty and Rewards process available?
<--- Score

46. What did the team gain from developing a sub-process map?
<--- Score

47. Do your employees have the opportunity to do what they do best everyday?
<--- Score

48. Is the gap/opportunity displayed and communicated in financial terms?
<--- Score

49. Did any additional data need to be collected?
<--- Score

50. Do you, as a leader, bounce back quickly from setbacks?
<--- Score

51. What are your key performance measures or indicators and in-process measures for the control and improvement of your Loyalty and Rewards processes?
<--- Score

52. What are your Loyalty and Rewards processes?
<--- Score

53. How do you identify specific Loyalty and Rewards investment opportunities and emerging trends?
<--- Score

54. How is the way you as the leader think and process information affecting your organizational culture?
<--- Score

55. What other jobs or tasks affect the performance of the steps in the Loyalty and Rewards process?
<--- Score

56. Was a detailed process map created to amplify critical steps of the 'as is' business process?
<--- Score

57. What are the revised rough estimates of the financial savings/opportunity for Loyalty and Rewards improvements?
<--- Score

58. Is the suppliers process defined and controlled?
<--- Score

59. What are your current levels and trends in key Loyalty and Rewards measures or indicators of

product and process performance that are important to and directly serve your customers?
<--- Score

60. What conclusions were drawn from the team's data collection and analysis? How did the team reach these conclusions?
<--- Score

61. How do mission and objectives affect the Loyalty and Rewards processes of your organization?
<--- Score

Add up total points for this section:
_ _ _ _ _ = Total points for this section

Divided by: _ _ _ _ _ _ (number of statements answered) = _ _ _ _ _ _
Average score for this section

Transfer your score to the Loyalty and Rewards Index at the beginning of the Self-Assessment.

CRITERION #5: IMPROVE:

INTENT: Develop a practical solution.
Innovate, establish and test the
solution and to measure the results.

In my belief, the answer to this
question is clearly defined:

5 Strongly Agree

4 Agree

3 Neutral

2 Disagree

1 Strongly Disagree

1. How do you keep improving Loyalty and Rewards?
<--- Score

2. How did the team generate the list of possible solutions?
<--- Score

3. Is there a small-scale pilot for proposed improvement(s)? What conclusions were drawn from

the outcomes of a pilot?
<--- Score

4. What tools were most useful during the improve phase?
<--- Score

5. What lessons, if any, from a pilot were incorporated into the design of the full-scale solution?
<--- Score

6. What resources are required for the improvement efforts?
<--- Score

7. How will the organization know that the solution worked?
<--- Score

8. Is supporting Loyalty and Rewards documentation required?
<--- Score

9. How does the team improve its work?
<--- Score

10. Is the optimal solution selected based on testing and analysis?
<--- Score

11. How do you measure progress and evaluate training effectiveness?
<--- Score

12. How will you know that you have improved?
<--- Score

13. What is Loyalty and Rewards's impact on utilizing the best solution(s)?
<--- Score

14. Do you cover the five essential competencies: Communication, Collaboration,Innovation, Adaptability, and Leadership that improve an organization's ability to leverage the new Loyalty and Rewards in a volatile global economy?
<--- Score

15. What tools were used to tap into the creativity and encourage 'outside the box' thinking?
<--- Score

16. What can you do to improve?
<--- Score

17. How do you improve productivity?
<--- Score

18. Who will be responsible for documenting the Loyalty and Rewards requirements in detail?
<--- Score

19. Is there a cost/benefit analysis of optimal solution(s)?
<--- Score

20. How can you improve Loyalty and Rewards?
<--- Score

21. What is the team's contingency plan for potential problems occurring in implementation?
<--- Score

22. What is the risk?
<--- Score

23. What were the underlying assumptions on the cost-benefit analysis?
<--- Score

24. What communications are necessary to support the implementation of the solution?
<--- Score

25. Who controls the risk?
<--- Score

26. Risk events: what are the things that could go wrong?
<--- Score

27. Is the measure of success for Loyalty and Rewards understandable to a variety of people?
<--- Score

28. What to do with the results or outcomes of measurements?
<--- Score

29. How do the Loyalty and Rewards results compare with the performance of your competitors and other organizations with similar offerings?
<--- Score

30. Explorations of the frontiers of Loyalty and Rewards will help you build influence, improve Loyalty and Rewards, optimize decision making, and sustain change, what is your approach?

<--- Score

31. How do you measure improved Loyalty and Rewards service perception, and satisfaction?
<--- Score

32. Are new and improved process ('should be') maps developed?
<--- Score

33. What is the magnitude of the improvements?
<--- Score

34. Is there a high likelihood that any recommendations will achieve their intended results?
<--- Score

35. What attendant changes will need to be made to ensure that the solution is successful?
<--- Score

36. For decision problems, how do you develop a decision statement?
<--- Score

37. How do you link measurement and risk?
<--- Score

38. What tools were used to evaluate the potential solutions?
<--- Score

39. What went well, what should change, what can improve?
<--- Score

40. Describe the design of the pilot and what tests were conducted, if any?
<--- Score

41. How do you improve Loyalty and Rewards service perception, and satisfaction?
<--- Score

42. For estimation problems, how do you develop an estimation statement?
<--- Score

43. What error proofing will be done to address some of the discrepancies observed in the 'as is' process?
<--- Score

44. Who are the people involved in developing and implementing Loyalty and Rewards?
<--- Score

45. What actually has to improve and by how much?
<--- Score

46. Do you combine technical expertise with business knowledge and Loyalty and Rewards Key topics include lifecycles, development approaches, requirements and how to make a business case?
<--- Score

47. In the past few months, what is the smallest change you have made that has had the biggest positive result? What was it about that small change that produced the large return?
<--- Score

48. What does the 'should be' process map/design

look like?
<--- Score

49. How does the solution remove the key sources of issues discovered in the analyze phase?
<--- Score

50. What improvements have been achieved?
<--- Score

51. How do you go about comparing Loyalty and Rewards approaches/solutions?
<--- Score

52. Are possible solutions generated and tested?
<--- Score

53. How can skill-level changes improve Loyalty and Rewards?
<--- Score

54. Were any criteria developed to assist the team in testing and evaluating potential solutions?
<--- Score

55. Who controls key decisions that will be made?
<--- Score

56. What are your current levels and trends in key measures or indicators of workforce and leader development?
<--- Score

57. What is the implementation plan?
<--- Score

58. If you could go back in time five years, what decision would you make differently? What is your best guess as to what decision you're making today you might regret five years from now?
<--- Score

59. How do you manage and improve your Loyalty and Rewards work systems to deliver customer value and achieve organizational success and sustainability?
<--- Score

60. Risk factors: what are the characteristics of Loyalty and Rewards that make it risky?
<--- Score

61. What needs improvement? Why?
<--- Score

62. Do those selected for the Loyalty and Rewards team have a good general understanding of what Loyalty and Rewards is all about?
<--- Score

63. Why improve in the first place?
<--- Score

64. Are you assessing Loyalty and Rewards and risk?
<--- Score

65. What is the Loyalty and Rewards's sustainability risk?
<--- Score

66. Is the implementation plan designed?
<--- Score

67. How will you measure the results?
<--- Score

68. How will you know that a change is an improvement?
<--- Score

69. How will the team or the process owner(s) monitor the implementation plan to see that it is working as intended?
<--- Score

70. Is a contingency plan established?
<--- Score

71. How do you improve your likelihood of success ?
<--- Score

72. What do you want to improve?
<--- Score

73. What are the implications of the one critical Loyalty and Rewards decision 10 minutes, 10 months, and 10 years from now?
<--- Score

74. At what point will vulnerability assessments be performed once Loyalty and Rewards is put into production (e.g., ongoing Risk Management after implementation)?
<--- Score

75. Is pilot data collected and analyzed?
<--- Score

76. What tools do you use once you have decided on

a Loyalty and Rewards strategy and more importantly how do you choose?
<--- Score

77. Is the solution technically practical?
<--- Score

78. How do you measure risk?
<--- Score

79. To what extent does management recognize Loyalty and Rewards as a tool to increase the results?
<--- Score

80. What should a proof of concept or pilot accomplish?
<--- Score

81. How will you know when its improved?
<--- Score

82. How significant is the improvement in the eyes of the end user?
<--- Score

83. Are there any constraints (technical, political, cultural, or otherwise) that would inhibit certain solutions?
<--- Score

84. Who will be responsible for making the decisions to include or exclude requested changes once Loyalty and Rewards is underway?
<--- Score

85. Was a pilot designed for the proposed solution(s)?

<--- Score

86. Is a solution implementation plan established, including schedule/work breakdown structure, resources, risk management plan, cost/budget, and control plan?
<--- Score

87. Does the goal represent a desired result that can be measured?
<--- Score

88. Can the solution be designed and implemented within an acceptable time period?
<--- Score

89. How can you improve performance?
<--- Score

90. Are improved process ('should be') maps modified based on pilot data and analysis?
<--- Score

91. How do you decide how much to remunerate an employee?
<--- Score

92. Who will be using the results of the measurement activities?
<--- Score

93. Are the best solutions selected?
<--- Score

Add up total points for this section:
_____ = Total points for this section

Divided by: _____ (number of
statements answered) = _____
Average score for this section

Transfer your score to the Loyalty and
Rewards Index at the beginning of the
Self-Assessment.

CRITERION #6: CONTROL:

INTENT: Implement the practical solution. Maintain the performance and correct possible complications.

In my belief, the answer to this question is clearly defined:

5 Strongly Agree

4 Agree

3 Neutral

2 Disagree

1 Strongly Disagree

1. Does a troubleshooting guide exist or is it needed?
<--- Score

2. Is there a Loyalty and Rewards Communication plan covering who needs to get what information when?
<--- Score

3. What are the critical parameters to watch?
<--- Score

4. Against what alternative is success being measured?
<--- Score

5. Implementation Planning- is a pilot needed to test the changes before a full roll out occurs?
<--- Score

6. Where do ideas that reach policy makers and planners as proposals for Loyalty and Rewards strengthening and reform actually originate?
<--- Score

7. What do you stand for--and what are you against?
<--- Score

8. How likely is the current Loyalty and Rewards plan to come in on schedule or on budget?
<--- Score

9. In the case of a Loyalty and Rewards project, the criteria for the audit derive from implementation objectives. an audit of a Loyalty and Rewards project involves assessing whether the recommendations outlined for implementation have been met. Can you track that any Loyalty and Rewards project is implemented as planned, and is it working?
<--- Score

10. What are your results for key measures or indicators of the accomplishment of your Loyalty and Rewards strategy and action plans, including building and strengthening core competencies?
<--- Score

11. What is your theory of human motivation, and how does your compensation plan fit with that view?
<--- Score

12. What can you control?
<--- Score

13. Is there a standardized process?
<--- Score

14. How will the day-to-day responsibilities for monitoring and continual improvement be transferred from the improvement team to the process owner?
<--- Score

15. What is the control/monitoring plan?
<--- Score

16. Are the planned controls working?
<--- Score

17. Do you monitor the effectiveness of your Loyalty and Rewards activities?
<--- Score

18. What are you attempting to measure/monitor?
<--- Score

19. How might the organization capture best practices and lessons learned so as to leverage improvements across the business?
<--- Score

20. How will report readings be checked to effectively monitor performance?

<--- Score

21. Do you monitor the Loyalty and Rewards decisions made and fine tune them as they evolve?
<--- Score

22. How will the process owner and team be able to hold the gains?
<--- Score

23. How will new or emerging customer needs/requirements be checked/communicated to orient the process toward meeting the new specifications and continually reducing variation?
<--- Score

24. How do you encourage people to take control and responsibility?
<--- Score

25. Will any special training be provided for results interpretation?
<--- Score

26. Are the planned controls in place?
<--- Score

27. How will input, process, and output variables be checked to detect for sub-optimal conditions?
<--- Score

28. What are the key elements of your Loyalty and Rewards performance improvement system, including your evaluation, organizational learning, and innovation processes?
<--- Score

29. Is a response plan established and deployed?
<--- Score

30. Who has control over resources?
<--- Score

31. Is there documentation that will support the successful operation of the improvement?
<--- Score

32. Who is the Loyalty and Rewards process owner?
<--- Score

33. What are the known security controls?
<--- Score

34. Are operating procedures consistent?
<--- Score

35. How do you establish and deploy modified action plans if circumstances require a shift in plans and rapid execution of new plans?
<--- Score

36. Are controls in place and consistently applied?
<--- Score

37. How do your controls stack up?
<--- Score

38. What is the best design framework for Loyalty and Rewards organization now that, in a post industrial-age if the top-down, command and control model is no longer relevant?
<--- Score

39. What quality tools were useful in the control phase?
<--- Score

40. Who will be in control?
<--- Score

41. Is reporting being used or needed?
<--- Score

42. Do the Loyalty and Rewards decisions you make today help people and the planet tomorrow?
<--- Score

43. Are documented procedures clear and easy to follow for the operators?
<--- Score

44. Does the Loyalty and Rewards performance meet the customer's requirements?
<--- Score

45. Do the decisions you make today help people and the planet tomorrow?
<--- Score

46. Is new knowledge gained imbedded in the response plan?
<--- Score

47. Is knowledge gained on process shared and institutionalized?
<--- Score

48. How do controls support value?

<--- Score

49. How can you best use all of your knowledge repositories to enhance learning and sharing?
<--- Score

50. What other areas of the organization might benefit from the Loyalty and Rewards team's improvements, knowledge, and learning?
<--- Score

51. Is there a documented and implemented monitoring plan?
<--- Score

52. Will existing staff require re-training, for example, to learn new business processes?
<--- Score

53. What should the next improvement project be that is related to Loyalty and Rewards?
<--- Score

54. How will the process owner verify improvement in present and future sigma levels, process capabilities?
<--- Score

55. Are new process steps, standards, and documentation ingrained into normal operations?
<--- Score

56. Does Loyalty and Rewards appropriately measure and monitor risk?
<--- Score

57. What other systems, operations, processes, and

infrastructures (hiring practices, staffing, training, incentives/rewards, metrics/dashboards/scorecards, etc.) need updates, additions, changes, or deletions in order to facilitate knowledge transfer and improvements?
<--- Score

58. Who controls critical resources?
<--- Score

59. Does job training on the documented procedures need to be part of the process team's education and training?
<--- Score

60. What should you measure to verify efficiency gains?
<--- Score

61. Has the improved process and its steps been standardized?
<--- Score

62. Are you measuring, monitoring and predicting Loyalty and Rewards activities to optimize operations and profitability, and enhancing outcomes?
<--- Score

63. Is there a recommended audit plan for routine surveillance inspections of Loyalty and Rewards's gains?
<--- Score

64. Is there a control plan in place for sustaining improvements (short and long-term)?
<--- Score

65. Does the response plan contain a definite closed loop continual improvement scheme (e.g., plan-do-check-act)?
<--- Score

66. You may have created your quality measures at a time when you lacked resources, technology wasn't up to the required standard, or low service levels were the industry norm. Have those circumstances changed?
<--- Score

67. Is a response plan in place for when the input, process, or output measures indicate an 'out-of-control' condition?
<--- Score

68. What is the recommended frequency of auditing?
<--- Score

69. Who sets the Loyalty and Rewards standards?
<--- Score

70. How is change control managed?
<--- Score

71. Are suggested corrective/restorative actions indicated on the response plan for known causes to problems that might surface?
<--- Score

72. What key inputs and outputs are being measured on an ongoing basis?
<--- Score

73. Is there a transfer of ownership and knowledge to process owner and process team tasked with the responsibilities.
<--- Score

74. How do you select, collect, align, and integrate Loyalty and Rewards data and information for tracking daily operations and overall organizational performance, including progress relative to strategic objectives and action plans?
<--- Score

75. What do you measure to verify effectiveness gains?
<--- Score

76. Are pertinent alerts monitored, analyzed and distributed to appropriate personnel?
<--- Score

77. Have new or revised work instructions resulted?
<--- Score

78. Are there documented procedures?
<--- Score

Add up total points for this section:
_____ = Total points for this section

Divided by: _____ (number of statements answered) = _____
Average score for this section

Transfer your score to the Loyalty and Rewards Index at the beginning of the Self-Assessment.

CRITERION #7: SUSTAIN:

1. What is your competitive advantage?
<--- Score

2. How will you insure seamless interoperability of Loyalty and Rewards moving forward?
<--- Score

3. What are the rules and assumptions your industry operates under? What if the opposite were true?
<--- Score

4. How do you maintain Loyalty and Rewards's Integrity?
<--- Score

5. Who else should you help?
<--- Score

6. What are the top 3 things at the forefront of your Loyalty and Rewards agendas for the next 3 years?
<--- Score

7. What happens if you do not have enough funding?
<--- Score

8. Are you using a design thinking approach and integrating Innovation, Loyalty and Rewards Experience, and Brand Value?
<--- Score

9. What counts that you are not counting?
<--- Score

10. If you do not follow, then how to lead?
<--- Score

11. Whom among your colleagues do you trust, and for what?
<--- Score

12. Can you maintain your growth without detracting from the factors that have contributed to your success?
<--- Score

13. What would have to be true for the option on the table to be the best possible choice?

<--- Score

14. Are assumptions made in Loyalty and Rewards stated explicitly?
<--- Score

15. Do you have the right people on the bus?
<--- Score

16. What are the gaps in your knowledge and experience?
<--- Score

17. What are the long-term Loyalty and Rewards goals?
<--- Score

18. What sources do you use to gather information for a Loyalty and Rewards study?
<--- Score

19. What are you challenging?
<--- Score

20. Who is responsible for Loyalty and Rewards?
<--- Score

21. What knowledge, skills and characteristics mark a good Loyalty and Rewards project manager?
<--- Score

22. How can you become more high-tech but still be high touch?
<--- Score

23. Are new benefits received and understood?

<--- Score

24. Which Loyalty and Rewards goals are the most important?
<--- Score

25. How do customers see your organization?
<--- Score

26. At what moment would you think; Will I get fired?
<--- Score

27. How do you lead with Loyalty and Rewards in mind?
<--- Score

28. Are you paying enough attention to the partners your company depends on to succeed?
<--- Score

29. Are the assumptions believable and achievable?
<--- Score

30. Why is Loyalty and Rewards important for you now?
<--- Score

31. Who, on the executive team or the board, has spoken to a customer recently?
<--- Score

32. How will you motivate the stakeholders with the least vested interest?
<--- Score

33. What happens when a new employee joins the

organization?
<--- Score

34. How can you become the company that would put you out of business?
<--- Score

35. How do you accomplish your long range Loyalty and Rewards goals?
<--- Score

36. How do you determine the key elements that affect Loyalty and Rewards workforce satisfaction, how are these elements determined for different workforce groups and segments?
<--- Score

37. Who is on the team?
<--- Score

38. What are current Loyalty and Rewards paradigms?
<--- Score

39. What is the estimated value of the project?
<--- Score

40. What is the funding source for this project?
<--- Score

41. Are you failing differently each time?
<--- Score

42. Who do you think the world wants your organization to be?
<--- Score

43. How do you listen to customers to obtain actionable information?
<--- Score

44. In the past year, what have you done (or could you have done) to increase the accurate perception of your company/brand as ethical and honest?
<--- Score

45. How much contingency will be available in the budget?
<--- Score

46. Can the schedule be done in the given time?
<--- Score

47. What is your BATNA (best alternative to a negotiated agreement)?
<--- Score

48. Is the Loyalty and Rewards organization completing tasks effectively and efficiently?
<--- Score

49. Would you rather sell to knowledgeable and informed customers or to uninformed customers?
<--- Score

50. Do you have enough freaky customers in your portfolio pushing you to the limit day in and day out?
<--- Score

51. What threat is Loyalty and Rewards addressing?
<--- Score

52. Why not do Loyalty and Rewards?

<--- Score

53. How do you deal with Loyalty and Rewards changes?
<--- Score

54. What have you done to protect your business from competitive encroachment?
<--- Score

55. How do you foster the skills, knowledge, talents, attributes, and characteristics you want to have?
<--- Score

56. What trophy do you want on your mantle?
<--- Score

57. How can you negotiate Loyalty and Rewards successfully with a stubborn boss, an irate client, or a deceitful coworker?
<--- Score

58. Is Loyalty and Rewards realistic, or are you setting yourself up for failure?
<--- Score

59. What business benefits will Loyalty and Rewards goals deliver if achieved?
<--- Score

60. How is business? Why?
<--- Score

61. Think of your Loyalty and Rewards project, what are the main functions?
<--- Score

62. How do you keep records, of what?
<--- Score

63. How do you go about securing Loyalty and Rewards?
<--- Score

64. Instead of going to current contacts for new ideas, what if you reconnected with dormant contacts-- the people you used to know? If you were going reactivate a dormant tie, who would it be?
<--- Score

65. What are internal and external Loyalty and Rewards relations?
<--- Score

66. Will it be accepted by users?
<--- Score

67. Are you satisfied with your current role? If not, what is missing from it?
<--- Score

68. Do you have past Loyalty and Rewards successes?
<--- Score

69. What is your question? Why?
<--- Score

70. If there were zero limitations, what would you do differently?
<--- Score

71. What would you recommend your friend do if he/

she were facing this dilemma?
<--- Score

72. What is the purpose of Loyalty and Rewards in relation to the mission?
<--- Score

73. Is maximizing Loyalty and Rewards protection the same as minimizing Loyalty and Rewards loss?
<--- Score

74. What is something you believe that nearly no one agrees with you on?
<--- Score

75. What are the business goals Loyalty and Rewards is aiming to achieve?
<--- Score

76. If you had to leave your organization for a year and the only communication you could have with employees/colleagues was a single paragraph, what would you write?
<--- Score

77. Who will provide the final approval of Loyalty and Rewards deliverables?
<--- Score

78. What is it like to work for you?
<--- Score

79. How do you track customer value, profitability or financial return, organizational success, and sustainability?
<--- Score

80. Who are four people whose careers you have enhanced?
<--- Score

81. What is the craziest thing you can do?
<--- Score

82. What may be the consequences for the performance of an organization if all stakeholders are not consulted regarding Loyalty and Rewards?
<--- Score

83. Among your stronger employees, how many see themselves at the company in three years? How many would leave for a 10 percent raise from another company?
<--- Score

84. Who is the main stakeholder, with ultimate responsibility for driving Loyalty and Rewards forward?
<--- Score

85. What Loyalty and Rewards skills are most important?
<--- Score

86. What will be the consequences to the stakeholder (financial, reputation etc) if Loyalty and Rewards does not go ahead or fails to deliver the objectives?
<--- Score

87. What one word do you want to own in the minds of your customers, employees, and partners?
<--- Score

88. Who have you, as a company, historically been when you've been at your best?
<--- Score

89. How likely is it that a customer would recommend your company to a friend or colleague?
<--- Score

90. Have new benefits been realized?
<--- Score

91. Do you say no to customers for no reason?
<--- Score

92. Will there be any necessary staff changes (redundancies or new hires)?
<--- Score

93. What is the source of the strategies for Loyalty and Rewards strengthening and reform?
<--- Score

94. Marketing budgets are tighter, consumers are more skeptical, and social media has changed forever the way we talk about Loyalty and Rewards. How do you gain traction?
<--- Score

95. What are the challenges?
<--- Score

96. What is a feasible sequencing of reform initiatives over time?
<--- Score

97. Is your strategy driving your strategy? Or is the way in which you allocate resources driving your strategy?
<--- Score

98. How do you foster innovation?
<--- Score

99. If your company went out of business tomorrow, would anyone who doesn't get a paycheck here care?
<--- Score

100. Did your employees make progress today?
<--- Score

101. Is there any existing Loyalty and Rewards governance structure?
<--- Score

102. What are the usability implications of Loyalty and Rewards actions?
<--- Score

103. If you got fired and a new hire took your place, what would she do different?
<--- Score

104. Do you have an implicit bias for capital investments over people investments?
<--- Score

105. How important is Loyalty and Rewards to the user organizations mission?
<--- Score

106. What are the success criteria that will indicate

that Loyalty and Rewards objectives have been met and the benefits delivered?
<--- Score

107. How do you ensure that implementations of Loyalty and Rewards products are done in a way that ensures safety?
<--- Score

108. If you had to rebuild your organization without any traditional competitive advantages (i.e., no killer a technology, promising research, innovative product/ service delivery model, etc.), how would your people have to approach their work and collaborate together in order to create the necessary conditions for success?
<--- Score

109. Who will manage the integration of tools?
<--- Score

110. Who will be responsible for deciding whether Loyalty and Rewards goes ahead or not after the initial investigations?
<--- Score

111. Is it economical; do you have the time and money?
<--- Score

112. How do senior leaders deploy your organizations vision and values through your leadership system, to the workforce, to key suppliers and partners, and to customers and other stakeholders, as appropriate?
<--- Score

113. Who uses your product in ways you never expected?
<--- Score

114. What are the short and long-term Loyalty and Rewards goals?
<--- Score

115. Have benefits been optimized with all key stakeholders?
<--- Score

116. What does your signature ensure?
<--- Score

117. What is your Loyalty and Rewards strategy?
<--- Score

118. Is a Loyalty and Rewards team work effort in place?
<--- Score

119. What are the potential basics of Loyalty and Rewards fraud?
<--- Score

120. How do you keep the momentum going?
<--- Score

121. What is the kind of project structure that would be appropriate for your Loyalty and Rewards project, should it be formal and complex, or can it be less formal and relatively simple?
<--- Score

122. Why should people listen to you?

<--- Score

123. Where can you break convention?
<--- Score

124. What are you trying to prove to yourself, and how might it be hijacking your life and business success?
<--- Score

125. What is an unauthorized commitment?
<--- Score

126. What new services of functionality will be implemented next with Loyalty and Rewards ?
<--- Score

127. Are the criteria for selecting recommendations stated?
<--- Score

128. How do you make it meaningful in connecting Loyalty and Rewards with what users do day-to-day?
<--- Score

129. Do you know what you are doing? And who do you call if you don't?
<--- Score

130. How do you engage the workforce, in addition to satisfying them?
<--- Score

131. How do you manage Loyalty and Rewards Knowledge Management (KM)?
<--- Score

132. Is the impact that Loyalty and Rewards has shown?
<--- Score

133. Who will determine interim and final deadlines?
<--- Score

134. What are the essentials of internal Loyalty and Rewards management?
<--- Score

135. Which individuals, teams or departments will be involved in Loyalty and Rewards?
<--- Score

136. What is effective Loyalty and Rewards?
<--- Score

137. Who is responsible for ensuring appropriate resources (time, people and money) are allocated to Loyalty and Rewards?
<--- Score

138. Is Loyalty and Rewards dependent on the successful delivery of a current project?
<--- Score

139. What is the range of capabilities?
<--- Score

140. How can you incorporate support to ensure safe and effective use of Loyalty and Rewards into the services that you provide?
<--- Score

141. Which functions and people interact with the

supplier and or customer?

<--- Score

142. Which models, tools and techniques are necessary?

<--- Score

143. What should you stop doing?

<--- Score

144. How do you assess the Loyalty and Rewards pitfalls that are inherent in implementing it?

<--- Score

145. If you weren't already in this business, would you enter it today? And if not, what are you going to do about it?

<--- Score

146. What trouble can you get into?

<--- Score

147. What do we do when new problems arise?

<--- Score

148. What are specific Loyalty and Rewards rules to follow?

<--- Score

149. What are strategies for increasing support and reducing opposition?

<--- Score

150. Are you making progress, and are you making progress as Loyalty and Rewards leaders?

<--- Score

151. When information truly is ubiquitous, when reach and connectivity are completely global, when computing resources are infinite, and when a whole new set of impossibilities are not only possible, but happening, what will that do to your business?
<--- Score

152. What management system can you use to leverage the Loyalty and Rewards experience, ideas, and concerns of the people closest to the work to be done?
<--- Score

153. How will you know that the Loyalty and Rewards project has been successful?
<--- Score

154. How will you ensure you get what you expected?
<--- Score

155. Who do we want your customers to become?
<--- Score

156. Are you relevant? Will you be relevant five years from now? Ten?
<--- Score

157. How are you doing compared to your industry?
<--- Score

158. How do you know if you are successful?
<--- Score

159. Who are the key stakeholders?
<--- Score

160. What did you miss in the interview for the worst hire you ever made?
<--- Score

161. If your customer were your grandmother, would you tell her to buy what you're selling?
<--- Score

162. What will drive Loyalty and Rewards change?
<--- Score

163. Why is it important to have senior management support for a Loyalty and Rewards project?
<--- Score

164. How do you stay inspired?
<--- Score

165. Is there any reason to believe the opposite of my current belief?
<--- Score

166. Operational - will it work?
<--- Score

167. Political -is anyone trying to undermine this project?
<--- Score

168. How do you govern and fulfill your societal responsibilities?
<--- Score

169. What is the overall business strategy?
<--- Score

170. Do you think you know, or do you know you know ?
<--- Score

171. What information is critical to your organization that your executives are ignoring?
<--- Score

172. What potential megatrends could make your business model obsolete?
<--- Score

173. How do you create buy-in?
<--- Score

174. Were lessons learned captured and communicated?
<--- Score

175. What are the key enablers to make this Loyalty and Rewards move?
<--- Score

176. How much does Loyalty and Rewards help?
<--- Score

177. Who do you want your customers to become?
<--- Score

178. What current systems have to be understood and/or changed?
<--- Score

179. How do you proactively clarify deliverables and Loyalty and Rewards quality expectations?

<--- Score

180. What are your most important goals for the strategic Loyalty and Rewards objectives?
<--- Score

181. What happens at your organization when people fail?
<--- Score

182. What is your formula for success in Loyalty and Rewards ?
<--- Score

183. Why do and why don't your customers like your organization?
<--- Score

184. How do senior leaders actions reflect a commitment to the organizations Loyalty and Rewards values?
<--- Score

185. Do you have the right capabilities and capacities?
<--- Score

186. How do you provide a safe environment -physically and emotionally?
<--- Score

187. Ask yourself: how would you do this work if you only had one staff member to do it?
<--- Score

188. To whom do you add value?
<--- Score

189. What kind of crime could a potential new hire have committed that would not only not disqualify him/her from being hired by your organization, but would actually indicate that he/she might be a particularly good fit?
<--- Score

190. If you were responsible for initiating and implementing major changes in your organization, what steps might you take to ensure acceptance of those changes?
<--- Score

191. In retrospect, of the projects that you pulled the plug on, what percent do you wish had been allowed to keep going, and what percent do you wish had ended earlier?
<--- Score

192. Why should you adopt a Loyalty and Rewards framework?
<--- Score

193. In a project to restructure Loyalty and Rewards outcomes, which stakeholders would you involve?
<--- Score

194. Are there any disadvantages to implementing Loyalty and Rewards? There might be some that are less obvious?
<--- Score

195. Has implementation been effective in reaching specified objectives so far?
<--- Score

196. What are the barriers to increased Loyalty and Rewards production?
<--- Score

197. How does Loyalty and Rewards integrate with other business initiatives?
<--- Score

198. Do you see more potential in people than they do in themselves?
<--- Score

199. What was the last experiment you ran?
<--- Score

200. What stupid rule would you most like to kill?
<--- Score

201. How do you cross-sell and up-sell your Loyalty and Rewards success?
<--- Score

202. Who is responsible for errors?
<--- Score

203. What role does communication play in the success or failure of a Loyalty and Rewards project?
<--- Score

204. How long will it take to change?
<--- Score

205. If no one would ever find out about your accomplishments, how would you lead differently?
<--- Score

206. Are you changing as fast as the world around you?
<--- Score

207. Do Loyalty and Rewards rules make a reasonable demand on a users capabilities?
<--- Score

208. Whose voice (department, ethnic group, women, older workers, etc) might you have missed hearing from in your company, and how might you amplify this voice to create positive momentum for your business?
<--- Score

209. Are you / should you be revolutionary or evolutionary?
<--- Score

Add up total points for this section:
_____ = Total points for this section

Divided by: _____ (number of statements answered) = _____
Average score for this section

Transfer your score to the Loyalty and Rewards Index at the beginning of the Self-Assessment.

Loyalty and Rewards and Managing Projects, Criteria for Project Managers:

1.0 Initiating Process Group: Loyalty and Rewards

1. What were things that you did well, but could improve, and how?

2. How to control and approve each phase?

3. During which stage of Risk planning are modeling techniques used to determine overall effects of risks on Loyalty and Rewards project objectives for high probability, high impact risks?

4. Although the Loyalty and Rewards project manager does not directly manage procurement and contracting activities, who does manage procurement and contracting activities in your organization then if not the PM?

5. If the risk event occurs, what will you do?

6. How well did the chosen processes produce the expected results?

7. How well defined and documented were the Loyalty and Rewards project management processes you chose to use?

8. The process to Manage Stakeholders is part of which process group?

9. Realistic - Are the desired results expressed in a way that the team will be motivated and believe that the required level of involvement will be obtained?

10. Information sharing?

11. Professionals want to know what is expected from them what are the deliverables?

12. Mitigate. What will you do to minimize the impact should the risk event occur?

13. How should their needs be met?

14. Have you evaluated the teams performance and asked for feedback?

15. At which CMMI level are software processes documented, standardized, and integrated into a standard to-be practiced process for your organization?

16. Do you understand the communication expectations for this Loyalty and Rewards project?

17. Do you understand the quality and control criteria that must be achieved for successful Loyalty and Rewards project completion?

18. Who are the Loyalty and Rewards project stakeholders?

19. How will it affect me?

20. The Loyalty and Rewards project Managers have maximum authority in which type of organization?

1.1 Project Charter: Loyalty and Rewards

21. Assumptions and Constraints: What assumptions were made in defining Loyalty and Rewards project?

22. Customer Benefits: What customer requirements does this Loyalty and Rewards project address?

23. Who are the stakeholders?

24. What are the deliverables?

25. How will you learn more about the process or system youre trying to improve?

26. How high should you set our goals?

27. Why the Improvements?

28. Why is it important?

29. Pop Quiz – Which are the same inputs as in the Loyalty and Rewards project Charter?

30. What's in it for you?

31. When?

32. Name and describe the elements that deal with providing the detail?

33. Why do you need to manage scope?

34. If finished, on what date did it finish?

35. Whose input and support will this Loyalty and Rewards project require?

36. Avoid costs, improve service, and/ or comply with a mandate?

37. Strategic Fit: What is the Strategic Initiative Identifier for this Loyalty and Rewards project?

38. Is time of the essence?

39. What are the assigned resources?

40. Dependent Loyalty and Rewards projects: What Loyalty and Rewards projects must be underway or completed before this Loyalty and Rewards project can be successful?

1.2 Stakeholder Register: Loyalty and Rewards

41. How much influence do they have on the Loyalty and Rewards project?

42. What are the major Loyalty and Rewards project milestones requiring communications or providing communications opportunities?

43. How should employers make their voices heard?

44. What opportunities exist to provide communications?

45. Who wants to talk about Security?

46. Is Your Organization Ready for Change?

47. What is the power of the stakeholder?

48. What & Why?

49. How Big is the Gap?

50. How will Reports Be Created?

51. Who is Managing Stakeholder Engagement?

1.3 Stakeholder Analysis Matrix: Loyalty and Rewards

52. Which conditions out of the control of the management are crucial to contribute for the achievement of the development objective?

53. Are you working on the right risks?

54. Insurmountable weaknesses?

55. Which conditions out of the control of the management are crucial for the achievement of the immediate objective?

56. Who is most dependent on the resources at stake?

57. Does the organization have bad debt or cash-flow problems?

58. Processes and systems, etc?

59. Who is directly responsible for decisions on issues important to the Loyalty and Rewards project?

60. Cultural, attitudinal, behavioural?

61. Which conditions out of the control of the management are crucial for the achievement of the outputs?

62. Where are mitigation costs factored in?

63. Guiding question: Who shall you involve in the making of the stakeholder map?

64. Lack of competitive strength?

65. Why do you care?

66. What tools would help us communicate?

67. What is the relationship among stakeholders?

68. Who are potential allies and opponents?

69. Continuity, supply chain robustness?

70. Is changing technology threatening our organizations position?

2.0 Planning Process Group: Loyalty and Rewards

71. Who are the Loyalty and Rewards project stakeholders?

72. What is the critical path for this Loyalty and Rewards project, and what is the duration of the critical path?

73. Contingency planning. If a risk event occurs, what will you do?

74. How does activity resource estimation affect activity duration estimation?

75. Have operating capacities been created and/or reinforced in partners?

76. What Do You Need to Do?

77. What should you do next?

78. Why is it important to determine activity sequencing on Loyalty and Rewards projects?

79. Why do IT Loyalty and Rewards projects fail?

80. What factors are contributing to progress or delay in the achievement of products and results?

81. Is the schedule for the set products being met?

82. To what extent do the intervention objectives and strategies of the Loyalty and Rewards project respond to the organizations plans?

83. Is the Loyalty and Rewards project making progress in helping to achieve the set results?

84. Did you read it correctly?

85. To what extent is the program helping to influence the organizations policy framework?

86. To what extent has a PMO contributed to raising the quality of the design of the Loyalty and Rewards project?

87. Mitigate. What will you do to minimize the impact should a risk event occur?

88. Loyalty and Rewards project Assessment; Why did you do this Loyalty and Rewards project?

89. How can you make your needs known?

90. Am I just doing busywork to pass the time?

2.1 Project Management Plan: Loyalty and Rewards

91. What happened during the process that you found interesting?

92. What data/reports/tools/etc. do your PMs need?

93. Will you add a schedule and diagram?

94. If the Loyalty and Rewards project management plan is a comprehensive document that guides you in Loyalty and Rewards project execution and control, then what should it NOT contain?

95. What is Loyalty and Rewards project Scope Management?

96. Are alternatives safe, functional, constructible, economical, reasonable and sustainable?

97. What if, for example, the positive direction and vision of the organization causes expected trends to change resulting in greater need than expected?

98. Are comparable cost estimates used for comparing, screening and selecting alternative plans, and has a reasonable cost estimate been developed for the recommended plan?

99. Do the proposed changes from the Loyalty and Rewards project include any significant risks to safety?

100. What should you drop in order to add something new?

101. Is the appropriate plan selected based on the organizations objectives and evaluation criteria expressed in Principles and Guidelines policies?

102. What worked well?

103. What data/reports/tools/etc. do program managers need?

104. Are there any client staffing expectations?

105. Are cost risk analysis methods applied to develop contingencies for the estimated total Loyalty and Rewards project costs?

106. Do there need to be organizational changes?

107. Why Change?

108. Are the proposed Loyalty and Rewards project purposes different than a previously authorized Loyalty and Rewards project?

109. Who Manages Integration?

2.2 Scope Management Plan: Loyalty and Rewards

110. Have the personnel with the necessary skills and competence been identified and has agreement for their participation in the Loyalty and Rewards project been reached with the appropriate management?

111. What are the risks that could significantly affect the schedule of the Loyalty and Rewards project?

112. Are risk oriented checklists used during risk identification?

113. Were Loyalty and Rewards project team members involved in detailed estimating and scheduling?

114. Are Loyalty and Rewards project contact logs kept up to date?

115. Does the detailed Loyalty and Rewards project plan identify individual responsibilities for the next 4–6 weeks?

116. Is the Steering Committee active in Loyalty and Rewards project oversight?

117. Are the schedule estimates reasonable given the Loyalty and Rewards project?

118. How do you know how you are doing?

119. Product – what are you trying to accomplish and

how will you know when you are finished?

120. Are updated Loyalty and Rewards project time & resource estimates reasonable based on the current Loyalty and Rewards project stage?

121. Are adequate resources provided for the quality assurance function?

122. Has appropriate allowance been made for the effect of the learning curve on all personnel joining the Loyalty and Rewards project who do not have the required prior industry, functional & technical expertise?

123. Are schedule deliverables actually delivered?

124. To whom will the deliverables be first presented for inspection and verification?

125. Has the business need been clearly defined?

126. Are corrective actions taken when actual results are substantially different from detailed Loyalty and Rewards project plan (variances)?

127. Is there a requirements change management processes in place?

128. Are individual tasks of reasonable time effort (8–40 hours)?

129. Describe how the deliverables will be verified against the Loyalty and Rewards project scope. To whom will the deliverables be first presented for inspection and verification?

2.3 Requirements Management Plan: Loyalty and Rewards

130. How will the requirements become prioritized?

131. How often will the reporting occur?

132. Will the contractors involved take full responsibility?

133. Who will initially review the Loyalty and Rewards project work or products to ensure it meets the applicable acceptance criteria?

134. Is any organizational data being used or stored?

135. How will requirements be managed?

136. Will you perform a Requirements Risk assessment and develop a plan to deal with risks?

137. Define the Help Desk model. Who will take full responsibility?

138. Business analysis scope?

139. Who will do the reporting and to whom will reports be delivered?

140. Do you really need to write this document at all?

141. Who will finally present the work or product(s) for acceptance?

142. How do you know that you have done this right?

143. How knowledgeable is the team in the proposed application area?

144. What is a problem?

145. Do you know which stakeholders will participate in the requirements effort?

146. Subject to Change Control?

147. Who will approve the requirements (and if multiple approvers, in what order)?

148. Why Manage Requirements?

149. Do you understand the role that each stakeholder will play in the requirements process?

2.4 Requirements Documentation: Loyalty and Rewards

150. Who provides requirements?

151. How will Requirements be documented and who signs off on them?

152. What are the attributes of a customer?

153. What will be the integration problems?

154. Can the requirement be changed without a large impact on other requirements?

155. What if the system wasn t implemented?

156. How will the proposed Loyalty and Rewards project help?

157. What images does it conjure?

158. What kind of entity is a problem ?

159. Is the requirement properly understood?

160. The problem with gathering requirements is right there in the word gathering. What images does it conjure?

161. If applicable; are there issues linked with the fact that this is an offshore Loyalty and Rewards project?

162. Is the requirement realistically testable?

163. Consistency. Are there any requirements conflicts?

164. Can the requirements be checked?

165. Are there legal issues?

166. What Can Tools Do For Us?

167. What is the risk associated with the technology?

168. What is Effective documentation?

169. Who is interacting with the system?

2.5 Requirements Traceability Matrix: Loyalty and Rewards

170. Do we have a clear understanding of all subcontracts in place?

171. What are the chronologies, contingencies, consequences, criteria?

172. How Do you Manage Scope?

173. Will you use a Requirements Traceability Matrix?

174. Why Do you Manage Scope?

175. Describe the process for approving requirements so they can be added to the traceability matrix and Loyalty and Rewards project work can be performed. Will the Loyalty and Rewards project requirements become approved in writing?

176. What is the WBS?

177. What percentage of Loyalty and Rewards projects are producing traceability matrices between requirements and other work products?

178. How will it affect the stakeholders personally in their career?

179. Is there a requirements traceability process in place?

180. Why use a WBS?

181. How small is small enough?

2.6 Project Scope Statement: Loyalty and Rewards

182. Are the meetings set up to have assigned note takers that will add action/issues to the issue list?

183. Has the Loyalty and Rewards project Scope Statement been reviewed as part of the baseline process?

184. Is the Loyalty and Rewards project Sponsor function identified and defined?

185. Will the Risk Plan be updated on a regular and frequent basis?

186. Where and How Does the Team Fit Within the Organization Structure?

187. Name the 2 elements of scope management that deal with concept development ?

188. Is the plan under configuration management?

189. Will there be documented contingency plans for the top 5-10 risks?

190. Have the reports to be produced, distributed, and filed been defined?

191. Once its defined, what is the stability of the Loyalty and Rewards project scope?

192. Change Management vs. Change Leadership - What's the Difference?

193. Will all Loyalty and Rewards project issues be unconditionally tracked through the issue resolution process?

194. Who will you recommend approve the change, and when do you recommend the change reviews occur?

195. Has the format for tracking and monitoring schedules and costs been defined?

196. Is this process communicated to the customer and team members?

197. Loyalty and Rewards project Lead, Team Lead, Solution Architect?

198. Have you been able to easily identify success criteria and create objective measurements for each of the Loyalty and Rewards project scopes goal statements?

199. Did your Loyalty and Rewards project ask for this?

200. How often will scope changes be reviewed?

2.7 Assumption and Constraint Log: Loyalty and Rewards

201. What is positive about the current process?

202. Are there standards for code development?

203. Are there cosmetic errors that hinder readability and comprehension?

204. Is this process still needed?

205. How can constraints be violated?

206. Does the Plan conform to standards?

207. After observing execution of process, is it in compliance with the documented Plan?

208. Diagrams and tables are included to explain complex concepts and increase overall readability?

209. Was the document/deliverable developed per the appropriate or required standards (for example, Institute of Electrical and Electronics Engineers standards)?

210. Model-building: What data-analytic strategies are useful when building proportional-hazards models?

211. What Threats might prevent us from getting there?

212. Are there unnecessary steps that are creating bottlenecks and/or causing people to wait?

213. Are there processes in place to ensure internal consistency between the source code components?

214. When can log be discarded?

215. What do you log?

216. What Strengths do you have?

217. Have the scope, objectives, costs, benefits and impacts been communicated to all involved and/or impacted stakeholders and work groups?

218. What would you gain if you spent time working to improve this process?

219. Have all stakeholders been identified?

220. Do the requirements meet the standards of correctness, completeness, consistency, accuracy, and readability?

2.8 Work Breakdown Structure: Loyalty and Rewards

221. How big is a work-package?

222. Who has to do it?

223. Where does it take place?

224. Why would you develop a Work Breakdown Structure?

225. Is it still viable?

226. What has to be done?

227. How much detail?

228. When would you develop a Work Breakdown Structure?

229. What is the probability of completing the Loyalty and Rewards project in less that xx days?

230. Is the Work breakdown Structure (WBS) defined and is the scope of the Loyalty and Rewards project clear with assigned deliverable owners?

231. Do you need another level?

232. What is the probability that the Loyalty and Rewards project duration will exceed xx weeks?

233. How Far Down?

234. How many levels?

235. Can you make it?

236. Why is it useful?

237. When do you stop?

238. When does it have to be done?

239. Is it a change in scope?

240. How will you and your Loyalty and Rewards project team define the Loyalty and Rewards projects scope and work breakdown structure?

2.9 WBS Dictionary: Loyalty and Rewards

241. The WBS is developed as part of a Joint Planning session. But how do you know that youve done this right?

242. Can the contractor substantiate work package and planning package budgets?

243. Are overhead budgets and costs being handled according to the disclosure statement when applicable, or otherwise properly classified (for example, engineering overhead, IR&D)?

244. Are retroactive changes to direct costs and indirect costs prohibited except for the correction of errors and routine accounting adjustments?

245. Are management actions taken to reduce indirect costs when there are significant adverse variances?

246. Are significant decision points, constraints, and interfaces identified as key milestones?

247. Is cost performance measurement at the point in time most suitable for the category of material involved, but no earlier than the time of actual receipt of material?

248. Budgeted cost for work performed?

249. Is all budget available as management reserve identified and excluded from the performance measurement baseline?

250. Are overhead cost budgets (or Loyalty and Rewards projections) established on a facility-wide basis at least annually for the life of the contract?

251. Are the bases and rates for allocating costs from each indirect pool consistently applied?

252. Do work packages reflect the actual way in which the work will be done and are they meaningful products or management-oriented subdivisions of a higher level element of work?

253. Are indirect costs charged to the appropriate indirect pools and incurring organization?

254. Are direct or indirect cost adjustments being accomplished according to accounting procedures acceptable to us?

255. Are meaningful indicators identified for use in measuring the status of cost and schedule performance?

256. The total budget for the contract (including estimates for authorized but unpriced work)?

257. Software specification, development, integration, and testing, licenses ?

258. Is undistributed budget limited to contract effort which cannot yet be planned to CWBS elements at or below the level specified for reporting to the

Government?

2.10 Schedule Management Plan: Loyalty and Rewards

259. Are all Vendor contracts closed out?

260. Are Vendor contract reports, reviews and visits conducted periodically?

261. What will be the final cost of the Loyalty and Rewards project if status quo is maintained?

262. Is there an approved case?

263. Are the processes for schedule assessment and analysis defined?

264. How does the proposed individual meet each requirement?

265. How are Loyalty and Rewards projects different from Operations?

266. Are Loyalty and Rewards project team members involved in detailed estimating and scheduling?

267. Define units of measurement for each resource. For example, are you referencing gallons or liters?

268. Is an industry recognized mechanized support tool(s) being used for Loyalty and Rewards project scheduling & tracking?

269. Do Loyalty and Rewards project teams & team

members report on status / activities / progress?

270. Does all Loyalty and Rewards project documentation reside in a common repository for easy access?

271. Are the results of quality assurance reviews provided to affected groups & individuals?

272. Are the people assigned to the Loyalty and Rewards project sufficiently qualified?

273. Does a documented Loyalty and Rewards project organizational policy & plan (i.e. governance model) exist?

274. Have reserves been created to address risks?

275. Is the assigned Loyalty and Rewards project manager a PMP (Certified Loyalty and Rewards project manager) and experienced?

276. Are all key components of a Quality Assurance Plan present?

277. Is PERT / Critical Path or equivalent methodology being used?

2.11 Activity List: Loyalty and Rewards

278. How can the Loyalty and Rewards project be displayed graphically to better visualize the activities?

279. How do you determine the late start (LS) for each activity?

280. Are the required resources available or need to be acquired?

281. When will the work be performed?

282. Who will perform the work?

283. What is the least expensive way to complete the Loyalty and Rewards project within 40 weeks?

284. What is the probability the Loyalty and Rewards project can be completed in xx weeks?

285. How difficult will it be to do specific activities on this Loyalty and Rewards project?

286. What are you counting on?

287. How should ongoing costs be monitored to try to keep the Loyalty and Rewards project within budget?

288. How much slack is available in the Loyalty and Rewards project?

289. What are the critical bottleneck activities?

290. When do the individual activities need to start and finish?

291. Is there anything planned that doesn t need to be here?

292. For other activities, how much delay can be tolerated?

293. What is the total time required to complete the Loyalty and Rewards project if no delays occur?

294. What Went Wrong?

295. Where will it be performed?

296. Should you include sub-activities?

2.12 Activity Attributes: Loyalty and Rewards

297. Time for overtime?

298. How many days do you need to complete the work scope with a limit of X number of resources?

299. Activity: Whats Missing?

300. Whats Missing?

301. How difficult will it be to complete specific activities on this Loyalty and Rewards project?

302. How Do you Manage Time?

303. Activity: Fair or Not Fair?

304. Which method produces the more accurate cost assignment?

305. Would you consider either of these activities an outlier?

306. Why?

307. How else could the items be grouped?

308. Are the required resources available?

309. Is there a trend during the year?

310. What is the organization s history in doing similar activities?

311. What conclusions/generalizations can you draw from this?

312. Can more resources be added?

313. How Much Activity Detail Is Required?

314. What activity do you think you should spend the most time on?

2.13 Milestone List: Loyalty and Rewards

315. Environmental effects?

316. Can you derive how soon can the whole Loyalty and Rewards project finish?

317. Political effects?

318. What background experience, skills, and strengths does the team bring to the company?

319. How difficult will it be to do specific activities on this Loyalty and Rewards project?

320. Information and research?

321. Do you foresee any technical risks or developmental challenges?

322. Describe the companys strengths and core competencies. What factors will make the company succeed?

323. New USPs?

324. Timescales, deadlines and pressures?

325. When will the Loyalty and Rewards project be complete?

326. Legislative effects?

327. How late can each activity be finished and started?

328. How will you get the word out to customers?

329. It is to be a narrative text providing the crucial aspects of your Loyalty and Rewards project proposal answering what, who, how, when and where?

330. What date will the task finish?

2.14 Network Diagram: Loyalty and Rewards

331. How difficult will it be to do specific activities on this Loyalty and Rewards project?

332. Are the Gantt Chart and/or Network Diagram updated periodically and used to assess the overall Loyalty and Rewards project timetable?

333. Are you on time?

334. Can you calculate the confidence level?

335. What job or jobs could run concurrently?

336. Where Do Schedules Come From?

337. What job or jobs precede it?

338. Exercise: What is the probability that the Loyalty and Rewards project duration will exceed xx weeks?

339. What must be completed before an activity can be started?

340. Where do you schedule uncertainty time?

341. What is the probability of completing the Loyalty and Rewards project in less that xx days?

342. What job or jobs follow it?

343. What are the Key Success Factors?

344. If the Loyalty and Rewards project network diagram cannot change but you have extra personnel resources, what is the BEST thing to do?

345. Which type of network diagram allows you to depict four types of dependencies?

346. What are the tools?

347. What activities must follow this activity?

348. Review the logical flow of the network diagram. Take a look at which activities you have first and then sequence the activities. Do they make sense?

2.15 Activity Resource Requirements: Loyalty and Rewards

349. Organizational Applicability?

350. What are constraints that you might find during the Human Resource Planning process?

351. Other support in specific areas?

352. When does Monitoring Begin?

353. Why do you do that?

354. Are there unresolved issues that need to be addressed?

355. Do you use tools like decomposition and rolling-wave planning to produce the activity list and other outputs?

356. Anything else?

357. How many signatures do you require on a check and does this match what is in your policy and procedures?

358. How do you handle petty cash?

359. Which logical relationship does the PDM use most often?

360. What is the Work Plan Standard?

2.16 Resource Breakdown Structure: Loyalty and Rewards

361. Which resources should be in the resource pool?

362. What Defines a Successful Loyalty and Rewards project?

363. Changes Based on Input from Stakeholders?

364. Goals for the Loyalty and Rewards project. What is each stakeholders desired outcome for the Loyalty and Rewards project?

365. Who needs what information?

366. What is the purpose of assigning and documenting responsibility?

367. Who delivers the information?

368. Why is this important?

369. What is the number one predictor of a groups productivity?

370. What Is Loyalty and Rewards project Communication Management?

371. Who will be used as a Loyalty and Rewards project team member?

372. What is the organizations history in doing similar

activities?

373. Why Do you Do It?

374. What Went Right?

375. Who is allowed to perform which functions?

376. Who is allowed to see what data about which resources?

2.17 Activity Duration Estimates: Loyalty and Rewards

377. How does a Loyalty and Rewards project life cycle differ from a product life cycle?

378. Does a process exist to determine the probability of risk events?

379. What type of contract was used and why?

380. Does the software appear easy to learn?

381. Under these circumstances what would be the best thing to do?

382. Are training needs identified when resources do not have the required skills to complete Loyalty and Rewards project activities?

383. Why do you think schedule issues often cause the most conflicts on Loyalty and Rewards projects?

384. Discuss the changes in the job market for information technology workers. How does the job market and current state of the economy affect human resource management?

385. Do an Internet search on earning PMP certification. Be sure to search for Yahoo Groups related to this topic. What are some of the options you found to help people prepare for the exam?

386. Do checklists exist that list frequently performed activities?

387. Are Loyalty and Rewards project activities decomposed into manageable components to ensure expected management control?

388. Which BEST describes how this affects the Loyalty and Rewards project?

389. (Cpi), and schedule performance index (spi) for the Loyalty and Rewards project?

390. Are changes to the scope managed according to defined procedures?

391. Are procedures defined for calculating cost estimates?

392. Which suggestions do you find most useful?

393. What are the main types of contracts if you do decide to outsource?

394. Are procedures defined by which the Loyalty and Rewards project scope may be changed?

395. Are measurement techniques employed to determine the potential impact of proposed changes?

2.18 Duration Estimating Worksheet: Loyalty and Rewards

396. What questions do you have?

397. What s Next?

398. When, then?

399. Value Pocket Identification & Quantification What Are Value Pockets?

400. What is your role?

401. What work will be included in the Loyalty and Rewards project?

402. What is the probability the Loyalty and Rewards project can be completed in 47 weeks?

403. Does the Loyalty and Rewards project provide innovative ways for Veterans to overcome obstacles or deliver better outcomes?

404. Can the Loyalty and Rewards project be constructed as planned?

405. Science = Process: Remember the Scientific Method?

406. How should ongoing costs be monitored to try to keep the Loyalty and Rewards project within budget?

407. Do any colleagues have experience with the company and/or RFPs?

408. What is the total time required to complete the Loyalty and Rewards project if no delays occur?

409. Will the Loyalty and Rewards project collaborate with the local community and leverage resources?

410. When does the organization expect to be able to complete it?

411. Define the work as completely as possible. What work will be included in the Loyalty and Rewards project?

412. What is Cost and Loyalty and Rewards project Cost Management?

2.19 Project Schedule: Loyalty and Rewards

413. Is the Loyalty and Rewards project schedule available for all Loyalty and Rewards project team members to review?

414. Eliminate unnecessary activities. Are there activities that came from a template or previous Loyalty and Rewards project that are not applicable on this phase of this Loyalty and Rewards project?

415. Why Time Management?

416. Is the structure for tracking the Loyalty and Rewards project schedule well defined and assigned to a specific individual?

417. Understand the constraints used in preparing the schedule. Are activities connected because logic dictates the order in which others occur?

418. How can you minimize or control changes to Loyalty and Rewards project schedules?

419. It allows the Loyalty and Rewards project to be delivered on schedule. How Do you Use Schedules?

420. But how do you know that youve done this right?

421. Have all Loyalty and Rewards project delays been adequately accounted for, communicated to all stakeholders and adjustments made in overall Loyalty

and Rewards project schedule?

422. How much slack is available in the Loyalty and Rewards project?

423. Does the condition or event threaten the Loyalty and Rewards projects objectives in any ways?

424. Are all remaining durations correct?

425. How long does a 12 month Loyalty and Rewards project take?

426. What documents, if any, will the subcontractor provide (eg Loyalty and Rewards project schedule, quality plan etc)?

427. Was the Loyalty and Rewards project schedule reviewed by all stakeholders and formally accepted?

428. Schedule/Cost Recovery?

429. Your best shot for providing estimations how complex/how much work does the activity require?

2.20 Cost Management Plan: Loyalty and Rewards

430. Staffing Requirements?

431. Is the schedule updated on a periodic basis?

432. What would some of the life cycle costs be?

433. Is a Stakeholder Management plan in place that covers topics?

434. Is there an on-going process in place to monitor Loyalty and Rewards project risks?

435. Are the payment terms being followed?

436. Cost estimate preparation – What cost estimates will be prepared during the Loyalty and Rewards project phases?

437. Is the communication plan being followed?

438. Has a structured approach been used to break work effort into manageable components (WBS)?

439. Is there anything unique in this Loyalty and Rewards project s scope statement that will affect resources?

440. Who should write the PEP?

441. Timeline and milestones?

442. Is there an onboarding process in place?

443. Are meeting objectives identified for each meeting?

444. Is the Loyalty and Rewards project Sponsor clearly communicating the Business Case or rationale for why this Loyalty and Rewards project is needed?

445. Are all payments made according to the contract(s)?

446. Have activity relationships and interdependencies within tasks been adequately identified?

447. Has a Quality Assurance Plan been developed for the Loyalty and Rewards project?

448. Were Loyalty and Rewards project team members involved in detailed estimating and scheduling?

2.21 Activity Cost Estimates: Loyalty and Rewards

449. Can you change our activities?

450. What were things that you did very well and want to do the same again on the next Loyalty and Rewards project?

451. Scope statement only direct or indirect costs as well?

452. Is there anything unique in this Loyalty and Rewards project s scope statement that will affect resources?

453. Were escalated issues resolved promptly?

454. What is Loyalty and Rewards project Cost Management?

455. Estimated cost?

456. What are the audit requirements?

457. Are cost subtotals needed?

458. What is included in indirect cost being allocated?

459. What is Procurement?

460. Eac -estimate at completion, what is the total job expected to cost?

461. What skill level is required to do the job?

462. How and when do you enter into Loyalty and Rewards project Procurement Management?

463. How Do you Manage Cost?

464. What is the last item a Loyalty and Rewards project manager must do to finalize Loyalty and Rewards project close-out?

465. One way to define activities is to consider how organization employees describe jobs to families and friends. You basically want to know, What do you do?

466. Who determines when the contractor is paid?

467. What were things that you need to improve?

468. What communication items need improvement?

2.22 Cost Estimating Worksheet: Loyalty and Rewards

469. Is the Loyalty and Rewards project responsive to community need?

470. What happens to any remaining funds not used?

471. What costs are to be estimated?

472. Will the Loyalty and Rewards project collaborate with the local community and leverage resources?

473. Who is best positioned to know and assist in identifying such factors?

474. Does the Loyalty and Rewards project provide innovative ways for stakeholders to overcome obstacles or deliver better outcomes?

475. Ask: are others positioned to know, are others credible, and will others cooperate?

476. What info is needed?

477. What is the estimated labor cost today based upon this information?

478. What will others want?

479. How will the results be shared and to whom?

480. What Can Be Included?

481. Can a trend be established from historical performance data on the selected measure and are the criteria for using trend analysis or forecasting methods met?

482. Is it feasible to establish a control group arrangement?

483. Identify the timeframe necessary to monitor progress and collect data to determine how the selected measure has changed?

484. What is the purpose of estimating?

485. What additional Loyalty and Rewards project(s) could be initiated as a result of this Loyalty and Rewards project?

2.23 Cost Baseline: Loyalty and Rewards

486. Are you meeting with your team regularly?

487. What is the organization s history in doing similar tasks?

488. Verify business objectives. Are others appropriate, and well-articulated?

489. When should cost estimates be developed?

490. Are you asking management for something as a result of this update?

491. How difficult will it be to do specific tasks on the Loyalty and Rewards project?

492. What Weaknesses do you have?

493. Does the suggested change request seem to represent a necessary enhancement to the product?

494. Is request in line with priorities?

495. Has the documentation relating to operation and maintenance of the product(s) or service(s) been delivered to, and accepted by, operations management?

496. Are procedures defined by which the cost baseline may be changed?

497. Have all approved changes to the schedule baseline been identified and impact on the Loyalty and Rewards project documented?

498. Loyalty and Rewards project Goals -should others be reconsidered?

499. On budget?

500. Definition of done can be traced back to the definitions of what are you providing to the customer in terms of deliverables?

501. Is there anything you need from upper management in order to be successful?

502. What is Cost and Loyalty and Rewards project Cost Management?

503. Has the Loyalty and Rewards project documentation been archived or otherwise disposed as described in the Loyalty and Rewards project communication plan?

2.24 Quality Management Plan: Loyalty and Rewards

504. What is the return on investment?

505. Were there any deficiencies / issues in prior years self-assessment?

506. Were the right locations/samples tested for the right parameters?

507. What does it do for me (or to me)?

508. Is there a Quality Management Plan?

509. What is quality and how will you ensure it?

510. How are training records kept?

511. How effectively was the Quality Management Plan applied during Loyalty and Rewards project Execution?

512. How is staff informed of proper reporting methods?

513. How is staff trained on the recording of field notes?

514. Modifications to the requirements?

515. How do you ensure that protocols are up to date?

516. How do you ensure that your sampling methods and procedures meet your data quality objectives?

517. What are your key performance measures/ indicators for tracking progress relative to your action plans?

518. With the Five Whys method, the team considers why the issue being explored occurred. Do others then take that initial answer and ask Why?

519. Have all involved stakeholders and work groups committed to the Loyalty and Rewards project?

520. How do senior leaders create an organizational focus on customers and other stakeholders?

521. What would be the next steps or what else should you do at this point?

522. Were there any deficiencies / issues identified in the prior years self-assessment?

523. Who gets results of work?

2.25 Quality Metrics: Loyalty and Rewards

524. How does one achieve stability?

525. What level of statistical confidence do you use?

526. Are there any open risk issues?

527. Is a risk containment plan in place?

528. Are documents on hand to provide explanations of privacy and confidentiality?

529. How do you communicate results and findings to upper management?

530. Can visual measures help us to filter visualizations of interest?

531. Were number of defects identified?

532. Are there already quality metrics available that detect nonlinear embeddings and trends similar to the users perception?

533. Is there a set of procedures to capture, analyze and act on quality metrics?

534. Have alternatives been defined in the event that failure occurs?

535. How can the effectiveness of each of the

activities be measured?

536. What is the benchmark?

537. What metrics do you measure?

538. Which report did you use to create the data you are submitting?

539. What forces exist that would cause them to change?

540. Are applicable standards referenced and available?

541. When is the security analysis testing complete?

542. Are quality metrics defined?

2.26 Process Improvement Plan: Loyalty and Rewards

543. How Do you Manage Quality?

544. Where are you now?

545. Are you Making Progress on the Improvement Framework?

546. If a Process Improvement Framework Is Being Used, Which Elements Will Help the Problems and Goals Listed?

547. What personnel are the coaches for your initiative?

548. Why Quality Management?

549. What personnel are the champions for the initiative?

550. Management commitment at all levels?

551. Has the time line required to move measurement results from the points of collection to databases or users been established?

552. Who should prepare the process improvement action plan?

553. Have the supporting tools been developed or acquired?

554. The motive is determined by asking, Why do I want to achieve this goal?

555. Modeling current processes is great, but will you ever see a return on that investment?

556. What personnel are the change agents for your initiative?

557. Are you following the quality standards?

558. To elicit goal statements, do you ask a question such as, What do you want to achieve?

559. Are you Making Progress on the Goals?

560. Are you meeting the quality standards?

561. What Actions Are Needed to Address the Problems and Achieve the Goals?

2.27 Responsibility Assignment Matrix: Loyalty and Rewards

562. Are authorized changes being incorporated in a timely manner?

563. Availability – will the group or the person be available within the necessary time interval?

564. Do others have the time to dedicate to your Loyalty and Rewards project?

565. Competencies and craftsmanship – what competencies are necessary and what level?

566. Do work packages consist of discrete tasks which are adequately described?

567. How do you manage remotely to staff in other Divisions?

568. Who is going to do that work?

569. What travel needed?

570. Which resource planning tool provides information on resource responsibility and accountability?

571. Is work properly classified as measured effort, LOE, or apportioned effort and appropriately separated?

572. Is cost and schedule performance measurement done in a consistent, systematic manner?

573. Are People Afraid to Let You Know When others Are Under Allocated?

574. The staff interests – is the group or the person interested in working for this Loyalty and Rewards project?

575. Does the Loyalty and Rewards project need to be analyzed further to uncover additional responsibilities?

576. Where does all this information come from?

577. Are all authorized tasks assigned to identified organizational elements?

578. Does the contractors system provide unit or lot costs when applicable?

2.28 Roles and Responsibilities: Loyalty and Rewards

579. Where are you most strong as a supervisor?

580. Be specific; avoid generalities. Thank you and great work alone are insufficient. What exactly do you appreciate and why?

581. Do you take the time to clearly define roles and responsibilities on Loyalty and Rewards project tasks?

582. Accountabilities: What are the roles and responsibilities of individual team members?

583. Is feedback clearly communicated and non-judgmental?

584. How well did the Loyalty and Rewards project Team understand the expectations of specific roles and responsibilities?

585. Are our budgets supportive of a culture of quality data?

586. Is the data complete?

587. Is there a training program in place for stakeholders covering expectations, roles and responsibilities and any addition knowledge others need to be good stakeholders?

588. Does our vision/mission support a culture of

quality data?

589. Are the quality assurance functions and related roles and responsibilities clearly defined?

590. Are governance roles and responsibilities documented?

591. Does the team have access to and ability to use data analysis tools?

592. Are Loyalty and Rewards project team roles and responsibilities identified and documented?

593. What should you do now to ensure that you are meeting all expectations of your current position?

594. How is your work-life balance?

595. Attainable / Achievable: The goal is attainable; can you actually accomplish the goal?

596. To decide whether to use a quality measurement, ask how will I know when it is achieved?

597. What areas of supervision are challenging for you?

598. Key conclusions and recommendations: Are conclusions and recommendations relevant and acceptable?

2.29 Human Resource Management Plan: Loyalty and Rewards

599. Does the schedule include Loyalty and Rewards project management time and change request analysis time?

600. Have all documents been archived in a Loyalty and Rewards project repository for each release?

601. Were Loyalty and Rewards project team members involved in the development of activity & task decomposition?

602. Are multiple estimation methods being employed?

603. How are you going to ensure that you have a well motivated workforce?

604. Is it standard practice to formally commit stakeholders to the Loyalty and Rewards project via agreements?

605. Are target dates established for each milestone deliverable?

606. Have external dependencies been captured in the schedule?

607. Does the Loyalty and Rewards project have a Quality Culture?

608. Are changes in deliverable commitments agreed to by all affected groups & individuals?

609. Loyalty and Rewards project Objectives?

610. Who Needs Training?

611. Are people motivated to meet the current and future challenges?

612. Are the right people being attracted and retained to meet the future challenges?

2.30 Communications Management Plan: Loyalty and Rewards

613. Which stakeholders can influence others?

614. Are the stakeholders getting the information others need, are others consulted, are concerns addressed?

615. In your work, how much time is spent on stakeholder identification?

616. What approaches to you feel are the best ones to use?

617. Who to share with?

618. What does the stakeholder need from the team?

619. How will the person responsible for executing the communication item be notified?

620. Which team member will work with each stakeholder?

621. Are others needed?

622. Do you have members of your team responsible for certain stakeholders?

623. Who to learn from?

624. What to learn?

625. Where do team members get information?

626. Who needs to know and how much?

627. Conflict Resolution -which method when?

628. What data is going to be required?

629. What approaches do you use?

630. Are there too many who have an interest in some aspect of your work?

631. Why Manage Stakeholders?

632. Do you ask; can you recommend others for me to talk with about this initiative?

2.31 Risk Management Plan: Loyalty and Rewards

633. Are the best people available?

634. Do the requirements require the creation of components that are unlike anything your organization has previously built?

635. What are the chances the risk event will occur?

636. Are end-users enthusiastically committed to the Loyalty and Rewards project and the system/product to be built?

637. What is the probability the risk avoidance strategy will be successful?

638. Does the Loyalty and Rewards project team have experience with the technology to be implemented?

639. Is the customer willing to establish rapid communication links with the developer?

640. What are the chances the event will occur?

641. Is the customer willing to commit significant time to the requirements gathering process?

642. What Will Drive Change?

643. For software; Are compilers and code generators available and suitable for the product to be built?

644. What can you do to minimize the impact if it does?

645. How much risk can you tolerate?

646. Do you have a consistent repeatable process that is actually used?

647. Can the risk be avoided by choosing a different alternative?

648. Financial risk: Can the organization afford to undertake the Loyalty and Rewards project?

649. Can the Loyalty and Rewards project proceed without assuming the risk?

650. Are Loyalty and Rewards project requirements stable?

651. What does a risk management program do?

2.32 Risk Register: Loyalty and Rewards

652. What risks might negatively or positively affect achieving the Loyalty and Rewards project objectives?

653. Financial risk -can the organization afford to undertake the Loyalty and Rewards project?

654. Are there other alternative controls that could be implemented?

655. Which key risks have ineffective responses or outstanding improvement actions?

656. Have other controls and solutions been implemented in other services which could be applied as an alternative to additional funding?

657. What could prevent us delivering on the strategic program objectives and what is being done to mitigate such issues?

658. What are the major risks facing the Loyalty and Rewards project?

659. What will be done?

660. What is the reason for current performance gaps and do the risks and opportunities identified previously explain this?

661. Severity Prediction?

662. Schedule Impact/Severity Estimated Range (workdays) Assume the event happens, what is the potential impact?

663. What is a Risk?

664. Are our objectives at risk?

665. Recovery actions - planned actions taken once a risk has occurred to allow you to move on. What should you do after?

666. How often will the Risk Management Plan and Risk Register be formally reviewed, and by whom?

667. What can be done about it?

668. What should you do now?

669. Is further information required before making a decision?

670. When will it happen?

2.33 Probability and Impact Assessment: Loyalty and Rewards

671. Do requirements put excessive performance constraints on the product?

672. Should the risk be taken at all?

673. Does the customer have a solid idea of what is required?

674. How much is the probability of a risk occurring?

675. Sensitivity Analysis -Which risks will have the most impact on the Loyalty and Rewards project?

676. What will be the likely political situation during the life of the Loyalty and Rewards project?

677. Do you have specific methods that you use for each phase of the process?

678. What are the tools and techniques used in managing the challenges faced?

679. What would be the effect of slippage?

680. Will there be an increase in the political conservatism?

681. Have decisions that should be left open because of inadequate information on technology been identified and responsibility assigned for reducing the

uncertainty?

682. Are formal technical reviews part of this process?

683. How would you assess the risk management process in the Loyalty and Rewards project?

684. Is security a central objective?

685. Would avoiding any of such impact the Loyalty and Rewards project's chance of success?

686. Are there new risks that mitigation strategies might introduce?

687. What are the levels of understanding of the future users of the outcome/results of this Loyalty and Rewards project?

688. Who will be in command to monitor and control the performance of the consortium members (consortium leader/client)?

689. Has something like this been done before?

2.34 Probability and Impact Matrix: Loyalty and Rewards

690. Are testing tools available and suitable?

691. How will the consumption pattern change?

692. What will be the environmental impact of the Loyalty and Rewards project?

693. Which is the BEST thing to do?

694. How is the Loyalty and Rewards project going to be managed?

695. Do the people have the right combinations of skills?

696. What are the probable external agencies to act as Loyalty and Rewards project manager?

697. Are the risk data timely and relevant?

698. Do end-users have realistic expectations?

699. Were there any Loyalty and Rewards projects similar to this one in existence?

700. Pay attention to the quality of the plans: is the content complete, or does it seem to be lacking detail?

701. Has the need for the Loyalty and Rewards project

been properly established?

702. What will be the likely political environment during the life of the Loyalty and Rewards project?

703. What are the uncertainties associated with the technology selected for the Loyalty and Rewards project?

704. Who is going to be the consortium leader?

705. Are tool mentors available?

706. Could others have been better mitigated?

707. Management -what contingency plans do you have if the risk becomes a reality?

708. Can the Loyalty and Rewards project proceed without assuming the risk?

2.35 Risk Data Sheet: Loyalty and Rewards

709. How do you handle product safely?

710. What is the chance that it will happen?

711. What actions can be taken to eliminate or remove risk?

712. Who has a vested interest in how you perform as an organization (our stakeholders)?

713. Are new hazards created?

714. Whom do you serve (customers)?

715. Risk of What?

716. What can YOU do?

717. Will revised controls lead to tolerable risk levels?

718. If it happens, what are the consequences?

719. What Do you Know?

720. Do effective diagnostic tests exist?

721. What can happen?

722. What are the main opportunities available to us that you should grab while you can?

723. What is the environment within which you operate (social trends, economic, community values, broad based participation, national directions etc.)?

724. What if client refuses?

725. Has the most cost-effective solution been chosen?

726. How reliable is the data source?

727. What is the likelihood of it happening?

728. Potential for Recurrence?

2.36 Procurement Management Plan: Loyalty and Rewards

729. Is documentation created for communication with the suppliers and Vendors?

730. Are there checklists created to determine if all quality processes are followed?

731. Has a Loyalty and Rewards project Communications Plan been developed?

732. Have all documents been archived in a Loyalty and Rewards project repository for each release?

733. Are milestone deliverables effectively tracked and compared to Loyalty and Rewards project plan?

734. Are the Loyalty and Rewards project team members located locally to the users/stakeholders?

735. What is a Loyalty and Rewards project Management Plan?

736. Are Loyalty and Rewards project team roles and responsibilities identified and documented?

737. Are the Loyalty and Rewards project plans updated on a frequent basis?

738. Are trade-offs between accepting the risk and mitigating the risk identified?

739. Are action items captured and managed?

740. What types of contracts will be used?

741. Is the Loyalty and Rewards project schedule available for all Loyalty and Rewards project team members to review?

742. Are updated Loyalty and Rewards project time & resource estimates reasonable based on the current Loyalty and Rewards project stage?

743. Is there any form of automated support for Issues Management?

744. Has the Loyalty and Rewards project manager been identified?

745. Are issues raised, assessed, actioned, and resolved in a timely and efficient manner?

2.37 Source Selection Criteria: Loyalty and Rewards

746. With the rapid changes in information technology, will media be readable in five or ten years?

747. When should debriefings be held and how should they be scheduled?

748. What Can Not Be Disclosed?

749. What are the guiding principles for developing an evaluation report?

750. What does an evaluation address and what does a sample resemble?

751. What are the guidelines regarding award without discussions?

752. What past performance information should be requested?

753. Can you prevent comparison of proposals?

754. What are the most common types of rating systems?

755. Is a cost realism analysis used?

756. Are there any specific considerations that precludes offers from being selected as the awardee?

757. Does your documentation identify why the team concurs or differs with reported performance from past performance report (CPARs, questionnaire responses, etc.)?

758. When is it appropriate to issue a Draft Request for Proposal (DRFP)?

759. How should oral presentations be prepared for?

760. What are the most critical evaluation criteria that prove to be tiebreakers in the evaluation of proposals?

761. What Source Selection software is your team using?

762. Team Leads: What is your process for assigning ratings?

763. What management structure does the organization consider as optimal for performing the contract?

764. What should a DRFP include?

765. Are discussions anticipated?

2.38 Stakeholder Management Plan: Loyalty and Rewards

766. Have process improvement efforts been completed before requirements efforts begin?

767. Are you meeting your customers expectations consistently?

768. Are the appropriate IT resources adequate to meet planned commitments?

769. Have the key functions and capabilities been defined and assigned to each release or iteration?

770. When would you develop a Loyalty and Rewards project Execution Plan?

771. Do Loyalty and Rewards project managers participating in the Loyalty and Rewards project know the Loyalty and Rewards projects true status first hand?

772. Are requirements management tracking tools and procedures in place?

773. Is there a formal set of procedures supporting Stakeholder Management?

774. Has a capability assessment been conducted?

775. Was your organizations estimating methodology being used and followed?

776. Contradictory information between document sections?

777. Are formal code reviews conducted?

778. Detail warranty and/or maintenance periods?

779. What other teams / processes would be impacted by changes to the current process, and how?

780. What inspection and testing is to be performed?

781. Are meeting minutes captured and sent out after the meeting?

782. What are their reporting requirements?

2.39 Change Management Plan: Loyalty and Rewards

783. How much change management is needed?

784. What new behaviours are required?

785. Who should be involved in developing a change management strategy?

786. What are the needs, priorities and special interests of the audience?

787. What are the essentials of the message?

788. How frequently should you repeat the message?

789. Why would a Loyalty and Rewards project run more smoothly when change management is emphasized from the beginning?

790. What are the responsibilities assigned to each role?

791. What method and medium would you use to announce a message?

792. What is the most cynical response it can receive?

793. When should a given message be communicated?

794. What is the worst thing that can happen if you

chose not to communicate this information?

795. Will the readiness criteria be met prior to the training roll out?

796. When to start change management?

797. Are there any restrictions on who can receive the communications?

798. How many people are required in each of the roles?

799. What new roles are needed?

800. Do there need to be new channels developed?

801. What skills, education, knowledge, or work experiences should the resources have for each identified competency?

802. Who might present the most resistance?

3.0 Executing Process Group: Loyalty and Rewards

803. What are the challenges Loyalty and Rewards project teams face?

804. Based on your Loyalty and Rewards project communication management plan, what worked well?

805. How Will You Know You Did It?

806. What are deliverables of your Loyalty and Rewards project?

807. What are the main parts of the scope statement?

808. What is in place for ensuring adequate change control on Loyalty and Rewards projects that involve outside contracts?

809. What is the difference between conceptual, application, and evaluative questions?

810. How is Loyalty and Rewards project performance information created and distributed?

811. What type of information goes in the quality assurance plan?

812. How can your organization use a weighted decision matrix to evaluate proposals as part of source selection?

813. On which process should team members spend the most time?

814. What are the main types of goods and services being outsourced?

815. How well did the chosen processes fit the needs of the Loyalty and Rewards project?

816. How does Loyalty and Rewards project management relate to other disciplines?

817. How could you control progress of your Loyalty and Rewards project?

818. What type of people would you want on your team?

819. Will new hardware or software be required for servers or client machines?

820. Could a new application negatively affect the current IT infrastructure?

821. How will professionals learn what is expected from them what the deliverables are?

3.1 Team Member Status Report: Loyalty and Rewards

822. Does the product, good, or service already exist within the organization?

823. Will the staff do training or is that done by a third party?

824. Are the products of the organization's Loyalty and Rewards projects meeting their customer's objectives?

825. How can you make it practical?

826. Do you have an Enterprise Loyalty and Rewards project Management Office (EPMO)?

827. How will Resource Planning be done?

828. Does the organization have the means (staff, money, contract, etc.) to produce or to acquire the product, good, or service?

829. Does every department have to have a Loyalty and Rewards project Manager on staff?

830. When a teams productivity and success depend on collaboration and the efficient flow of information, what generally fails them?

831. Is there evidence that staff is taking a more professional approach toward management of the

organizations Loyalty and Rewards projects?

832. How it is to be done?

833. What is to be done?

834. The problem with Reward & Recognition Programs is that the truly deserving people all too often get left out. How can you make it practical?

835. How does this product, good, or service meet the needs of the Loyalty and Rewards project and the organization as a whole?

836. What specific interest groups do you have in place?

837. Why is it to be done?

838. How much risk is involved?

839. Are the attitudes of staff regarding Loyalty and Rewards project work improving?

840. Are the organization's Loyalty and Rewards projects more successful over time?

3.2 Change Request: Loyalty and Rewards

841. How is the change documented (format, content, storage)?

842. Who needs to approve change requests?

843. What are the duties of the change control team?

844. How does a team identify the discrete elements of a configuration?

845. Why were my requested changes rejected or not made?

846. What is the relationship between requirements attributes and attributes like complexity and size?

847. What are the requirements for urgent changes?

848. Who can suggest changes?

849. Will there be a change request form in use?

850. What has an inspector to inspect and to check?

851. How does an organization control changes before and after software is released to a customer?

852. What is a Change Request Form?

853. Will new change requests be acknowledged in a

timely manner?

854. When to Submit a Change Request?

855. Which requirements attributes affect the risk to reliability the most?

856. Should a more thorough impact analysis be conducted?

857. How can changes be graded?

858. What are the Impacts to an organization?

859. When Do you Create a Change Request?

860. Why do you want to have a change control system?

3.3 Change Log: Loyalty and Rewards

861. Will the Loyalty and Rewards project fail if the change request is not executed?

862. Is the requested change request a result of changes in other Loyalty and Rewards project(s)?

863. Do the described changes impact on the integrity or security of the system?

864. Is the change request open, closed or pending?

865. How does this change affect scope?

866. How does this relate to the standards developed for specific business processes?

867. When was the request approved?

868. How does this change affect the timeline of the schedule?

869. Is the submitted change a new change or a modification of a previously approved change?

870. Is the change request within Loyalty and Rewards project scope?

871. Is this a mandatory replacement?

872. Is the change backward compatible without limitations?

873. Does the suggested change request represent a desired enhancement to the products functionality?

874. Who initiated the change request?

875. Where Do Changes Come From?

876. When was the request submitted?

3.4 Decision Log: Loyalty and Rewards

877. What was the rationale for the decision?

878. Behaviors; what are guidelines that the team has identified that will assist them with getting the most out of their team meetings?

879. What eDiscovery problem or issue did your company set out to fix or make better?

880. Is your opponent open to a non-traditional workflow, or will it likely challenge anything you do?

881. How does provision of information, both in terms of content and presentation, influence acceptance of alternative strategies?

882. How do you define success?

883. What alternatives/risks were considered?

884. Do strategies and tactics aimed at less than full control reduce the costs of management or simply shift the cost burden?

885. What is the average size of your matters in an applicable measurement?

886. At what point in time does loss become unacceptable?

887. Is everything working as expected?

888. How effective is maintaining the log at facilitating organizational learning?

889. Adversarial Environment. Is your opponent open to a non-traditional workflow, or will it likely challenge anything you do?

890. Does anything need to be adjusted?

891. How do you know when you are achieving it?

892. How does the use a Decision Support System influence the strategies/tactics or costs?

893. Who is the decisionmaker?

894. How consolidated and comprehensive a story can we tell by capturing currently available incident data in a central location and through a log of key decisions during an incident?

895. Decision-making process; how will the team make decisions?

896. Which variables make a critical difference?

3.5 Quality Audit: Loyalty and Rewards

897. How does the organization know that its system for supporting staff research capability is appropriately effective and constructive?

898. How well do you think the organization engages with the outside community?

899. Do the suppliers use a formal quality system?

900. How does the organization know that its staff placements are appropriately effective and constructive in relation to program-related learning outcomes?

901. How does the organization know that its promotions system is appropriately effective, constructive and fair?

902. How does the organization know that its systems for communicating with and among staff are appropriately effective and constructive?

903. How does the organization know that its system for commercializing research outputs is appropriately effective and constructive?

904. How does the organization know that its staff entrance standards are appropriately effective and constructive and being implemented consistently?

905. How does the organization know that its management of its ethical responsibilities is appropriately effective and constructive?

906. How does the organization know that its general support services planning and management systems are appropriately effective and constructive?

907. Are all areas associated with the storage and reconditioning of devices clean, free of rubbish, adequately ventilated and in good repair?

908. What review processes are in place for the organizations major activities?

909. Are there appropriate indicators for monitoring the effectiveness and efficiency of processes?

910. How does the organization know that its relationships with relevant professional bodies are appropriately effective and constructive?

911. Quality is about improvement and accountability. The immediate questions that arise out of that statement are: (i) improvement on what, and (ii) accountable to whom?

912. Are storage areas and reconditioning operations designed to prevent mix-ups and assure orderly handling of both the distressed and reconditioned devices?

913. How does the organization know that its security arrangements are appropriately effective and constructive?

914. How does the organization know that its staff embody the core knowledge, skills and characteristics for which it wishes to be recognized?

915. How does the organization know that its system for maintaining and advancing the capabilities of its staff, particularly in relation to the Mission of the organization, is appropriately effective and constructive?

916. How does the organization know that its systems for providing high quality consultancy services to external parties are appropriately effective and constructive?

3.6 Team Directory: Loyalty and Rewards

917. Who will write the meeting minutes and distribute?

918. Process Decisions: Which organizational elements and which individuals will be assigned management functions?

919. Where will the product be used and/or delivered or built when appropriate?

920. Does a Loyalty and Rewards project team directory list all resources assigned to the Loyalty and Rewards project?

921. What are you going to deliver or accomplish?

922. Have you decided when to celebrate the Loyalty and Rewards projects completion date?

923. When will you produce deliverables?

924. Why is the work necessary?

925. Who will talk to the customer?

926. Process Decisions: Are there any statutory or regulatory issues relevant to the timely execution of work?

927. Who will report Loyalty and Rewards project

status to all stakeholders?

928. Where should the information be distributed?

929. Contract requirements complied with?

930. Process Decisions: Are all issues being addressed to the satisfaction of both parties within approximately 30 days from the time the issue is identified?

931. Process Decisions: Is work progressing on schedule and per contract requirements?

932. Decisions: Is the most suitable form of contract being used?

933. How do unidentified risks impact the outcome of the Loyalty and Rewards project?

934. What needs to be communicated?

935. Who are the Team Members?

936. How will you accomplish and manage the objectives?

3.7 Team Operating Agreement: Loyalty and Rewards

937. Are there more than two national cultures represented by your team?

938. What are the current caseload numbers in the unit?

939. Do you listen for voice tone and word choice to understand the meaning behind words?

940. How will group handle unplanned absences?

941. Have you established procedures that team members can follow to work effectively together, such as a team operating agreement?

942. How will you divide work equitably?

943. Methodologies: How will key team processes be implemented, such as training, research, work deliverable production, review and approval processes, knowledge management, and meeting procedures?

944. Do you use a parking lot for any items that are important but outside of the agenda?

945. Do you leverage technology engagement tools group chat, polls, screen sharing, etc.?

946. What is Teaming?

947. Do you post meeting notes and the recording (if used) and notify participants?

948. How does teaming fit in with overall organizational goals and meet organizational needs?

949. Did you prepare participants for the next meeting?

950. Do you brief absent members after they view meeting notes or listen to a recording?

951. Reimbursements: How will the team members be reimbursed for expenses and time commitments?

952. What is the number of cases currently teamed?

953. Are there the right people on your team?

954. Are leadership responsibilities shared among team members (versus a single leader)?

955. What is Culture?

956. Does your team need access to all documents and information at all times?

3.8 Team Performance Assessment: Loyalty and Rewards

957. If you have received criticism from reviewers that your work suffered from method variance, what was the circumstance?

958. To what degree is there a sense that only the team can succeed?

959. To what degree will the team adopt a concrete, clearly understood, and agreed-upon approach that will result in achievement of the teams goals?

960. How does Loyalty and Rewards project termination impact Loyalty and Rewards project team members?

961. To what degree will new and supplemental skills be introduced as the need is recognized?

962. What structural changes have you made or are you preparing to make?

963. To what degree does the teams work approach provide opportunity for members to engage in fact-based problem solving?

964. To what degree do members understand and articulate the same purpose without relying on ambiguous abstractions?

965. To what degree do team members understand

one anothers roles and skills?

966. Effects of crew composition on crew performance: Does the whole equal the sum of its parts?

967. To what degree are the skill areas critical to team performance present?

968. What are Teams?

969. Does more radicalness mean more perceived benefits?

970. To what degree are sub-teams possible or necessary?

971. What are you doing specifically to develop the leaders around you?

972. To what degree are these categories of skills either actually or potentially represented across the membership?

973. Social categorization and intergroup behaviour: Does minimal intergroup discrimination make social identity more positive?

974. How do you keep key people outside the group informed about its accomplishments?

975. When a reviewer complains about method variance, what is the essence of the complaint?

976. To what degree can team members frequently and easily communicate with one another?

3.9 Team Member Performance Assessment: Loyalty and Rewards

977. What is the target group for instruction (e.g., individual and collective or small team instruction)?

978. What are the evaluation strategies (e.g., reaction, learning, behavior, results) used. What evaluation results did you have?

979. What is used as a basis for instructional decisions?

980. Who they are?

981. To what degree do members articulate the goals beyond the team membership?

982. What are they responsible for?

983. Do the goals support the organizations goals?

984. How was the determination made for which training platforms would be used (i.e., media selection)?

985. What is collaboration?

986. What evidence supports your decision-making?

987. What are the basic principles and objectives of performance measurement and assessment?

988. Are any validation activities performed?

989. How is assessment information achieved, stored?

990. Are any governance changes sufficient to impact achievement?

991. How do you determine which data are the most important to use, analyze, or review?

992. To what degree are the goals realistic?

993. How do you work together to improve teaching and learning?

994. To what degree do team members frequently explore the teams purpose and its implications?

995. What are best practices for delivering and developing training evaluations to maximize the benefits of leveraging emerging technologies?

996. Are there any safeguards to prevent intentional or unintentional rating errors?

3.10 Issue Log: Loyalty and Rewards

997. Who are the members of the governing body?

998. What is the impact on the Business Case?

999. What would have to change?

1000. What is the stakeholders level of authority?

1001. Do you feel more overwhelmed by stakeholders?

1002. What help do you and your team need from the stakeholders?

1003. Do you often overlook a key stakeholder or stakeholder group?

1004. How were past initiatives successful?

1005. Can an impact cause deviation beyond team, stage or Loyalty and Rewards project tolerances?

1006. What are the stakeholders interrelationships?

1007. How do you reply to this question; I am new here and managing this major program. How do you suggest I build my network?

1008. Is there an important stakeholder who is actively opposed and will not receive messages?

1009. Why Multiple Evaluators?

1010. How Do you Manage Communications?

1011. How much time does it take to do it?

1012. Is access to the Issue Log controlled?

1013. Is the Issue Log kept in a safe place?

4.0 Monitoring and Controlling Process Group: Loyalty and Rewards

1014. What areas were overlooked on this Loyalty and Rewards project?

1015. Is the verbiage used appropriate and understandable?

1016. What do they need to know about the Loyalty and Rewards project?

1017. What good practices or successful experiences or transferable examples have been identified?

1018. Based on your Loyalty and Rewards project communication management plan, what worked well?

1019. When will the Loyalty and Rewards project be done?

1020. Feasibility: How much money, time, and effort can you put into this?

1021. Is there sufficient time allotted between the general system design and the detailed system design phases?

1022. How are you doing?

1023. Is progress on outcomes due to your program?

1024. What areas does the group agree are the biggest success on the Loyalty and Rewards project?

1025. What resources are necessary?

1026. Are the necessary foundations in place to ensure the sustainability of the results of the programme?

1027. What were things that you did very well and want to do the same again on the next Loyalty and Rewards project?

1028. How to ensure validity, quality and consistency?

1029. What Business Situation Is Being Addressed?

1030. Accuracy: What design will lead to accurate information?

4.1 Project Performance Report: Loyalty and Rewards

1031. What is in it for you?

1032. How can Loyalty and Rewards project Sustainability be Maintained?

1033. To what degree can the team measure progress against specific goals?

1034. To what degree do the goals specify concrete team work products?

1035. To what degree will the team adopt a concrete, clearly understood, and agreed-upon approach that will result in achievement of the team's goals?

1036. To what degree does the information network provide individuals with the information they require?

1037. To what degree do team members feel that the purpose of the team is important, if not exciting?

1038. To what degree does the team's work approach provide opportunity for members to engage in open interaction?

1039. To what degree is the team cognizant of small wins to be celebrated along the way?

1040. To what degree are fresh input and perspectives systematically caught and added (for example, through information and analysis, new members, and senior sponsors)?

1041. To what degree do all members feel responsible for all agreed-upon measures?

1042. To what degree is the information network consistent with the structure of the formal organization?

1043. To what degree does the team's approach to its work allow for modification and improvement over time?

1044. To what degree does the team's purpose constitute a broader, deeper aspiration than just accomplishing short-term goals?

1045. To what degree does the formal organization make use of individual resources and meet individual needs?

1046. To what degree will each member have the opportunity to advance his or her professional skills in all three of the above categories while contributing to the accomplishment of the team's purpose and goals?

1047. To what degree does the task meet individual needs?

1048. To what degree is there centralized control of information sharing?

1049. What is the degree to which rules govern information exchange between groups?

4.2 Variance Analysis: Loyalty and Rewards

1050. Wbs elements contractually specified for reporting of status to the organization (lowest level only)?

1051. Are indirect costs accumulated for comparison with the corresponding budgets?

1052. Is there a logical explanation for any variance?

1053. How do you verify authorization to proceed with all authorized work?

1054. How do you evaluate the impact of schedule changes, work around, et?

1055. Are the requirements for all items of overhead established by rational, traceable processes?

1056. How does the monthly budget compare to the actual experience?

1057. What is the expected future profitability of each customer?

1058. Are overhead costs budgets established on a basis consistent with the anticipated direct business base?

1059. Budget versus Actual. How does the monthly budget compare to actual experience?

1060. Historical experience?

1061. Are control accounts opened and closed based on the start and completion of work contained therein?

1062. How do you manage changes in the nature of the overhead requirements?

1063. The anticipated business volume?

1064. Are all budgets assigned to control accounts?

1065. Are the WBS and organizational levels for application of the Loyalty and Rewards projected overhead costs identified?

1066. What is the actual cost of work performed?

4.3 Earned Value Status: Loyalty and Rewards

1067. How does this compare with other Loyalty and Rewards projects?

1068. When is it going to finish?

1069. How much is it going to cost by the finish?

1070. If earned value management (EVM) is so good in determining the true status of a Loyalty and Rewards project and Loyalty and Rewards project its completion, why is it that hardly any one uses it in information systems related Loyalty and Rewards projects?

1071. Validation is a process of ensuring that the developed system will actually achieve the stakeholders desired outcomes; Are you building the right product? What do you validate?

1072. Where are your problem areas?

1073. Verification is a process of ensuring that the developed system satisfies the stakeholders agreements and specifications; Are you building the product right? What do you verify?

1074. Earned Value can be used in almost any Loyalty and Rewards project situation and in almost any Loyalty and Rewards project environment. It may be used on large Loyalty and Rewards projects, medium sized Loyalty and Rewards projects, tiny Loyalty and Rewards projects (in cut-down form), complex and simple Loyalty and Rewards projects and in any market sector. Some people, of course, know all about earned value, they have used it for years - but perhaps not as effectively as they could have?

1075. Where is Evidence-based Earned Value in your organization reported?

1076. What is the unit of forecast value?

1077. Are you hitting your Loyalty and Rewards projects targets?

4.4 Risk Audit: Loyalty and Rewards

1078. Is the organization willing to commit significant time to the requirements gathering process?

1079. Do you have an emergency plan?

1080. How effective are your risk controls?

1081. Are all managers or operators of the facility or equipment competent or qualified?

1082. Are Loyalty and Rewards project requirements stable?

1083. Are requirements fully understood by the team and their customers?

1084. Who audits the auditor?

1085. Are end-users enthusiastically committed to the Loyalty and Rewards project and the system/product to be built?

1086. Do you have financial policies and procedures in place to guide officers of the organization/treasurer/ general members?

1087. What are the risks that could stop you from achieving your KPIs?

1088. Are all participants informed of safety issues?

1089. Are procedures in place to ensure the security

of staff and information and compliance with privacy legislation if applicable?

1090. Improving Fraud Detection: Do Auditors React to Abnormal Inconsistencies between Financial and Non-financial Measures?

1091. How do you prioritize risks?

1092. Do you have position descriptions for all key paid and volunteer positions in your organization?

1093. How will you maximise opportunities?

1094. Do your financial policies and procedures ensure that each step in financial handling (receipt, recording, banking, reporting) is not completed by one person?

1095. What are the commonly used work arounds in high risk areas?

1096. Are some people working on multiple Loyalty and Rewards projects?

4.5 Contractor Status Report: Loyalty and Rewards

1097. Who can list a Loyalty and Rewards project as company experience, the company or a previous employee of the company?

1098. How long have you been using the services?

1099. What was the overall budget or estimated cost?

1100. Are there contractual transfer concerns?

1101. What was the final actual cost?

1102. Describe how often regular updates are made to the proposed solution. Are these regular updates included in the standard maintenance plan?

1103. What was the actual budget or estimated cost for your companys services?

1104. What was the budget or estimated cost for your companys services?

1105. How is Risk Transferred?

1106. If applicable; describe your standard schedule for new software version releases. Are new software version releases included in the standard maintenance plan?

1107. What is the average response time for

answering a support call?

1108. What are the minimum and optimal bandwidth requirements for the proposed soluiton?

1109. What process manages the contracts?

4.6 Formal Acceptance: Loyalty and Rewards

1110. Did the Loyalty and Rewards project manager and team act in a professional and ethical manner?

1111. Was the Loyalty and Rewards project goal achieved?

1112. Do you perform formal acceptance or burn-in tests?

1113. Was the Loyalty and Rewards project work done on time, within budget, and according to specification?

1114. General estimate of the costs and times to complete the Loyalty and Rewards project?

1115. Do you buy-in installation services?

1116. Was the sponsor/customer satisfied?

1117. Was the Loyalty and Rewards project managed well?

1118. Does it do what Loyalty and Rewards project team said it would?

1119. What was done right?

1120. What features, practices, and processes proved to be strengths or weaknesses?

1121. What are the requirements against which to test, Who will execute?

1122. Does it do what client said it would?

1123. What function(s) does it fill or meet?

1124. Do you buy pre-configured systems or build your own configuration?

1125. Who supplies data?

1126. What lessons were learned about your Loyalty and Rewards project management methodology?

1127. What can you do better next time?

1128. How well did the team follow the methodology?

1129. Is formal acceptance of the Loyalty and Rewards project product documented and distributed?

5.0 Closing Process Group: Loyalty and Rewards

1130. Were the outcomes different from those planned?

1131. Did you do what you said you were going to do?

1132. What areas does the group agree are the biggest success on the Loyalty and Rewards project?

1133. What were the desired outcomes?

1134. How well did the chosen processes fit the needs of the Loyalty and Rewards project?

1135. If a risk event occurs, what will you do?

1136. What were things that you did very well and want to do the same again on the next Loyalty and Rewards project?

1137. What is the Loyalty and Rewards project Management Process?

1138. Was the schedule met?

1139. What can you do better next time, and what specific actions can you take to improve?

1140. How well did the team follow the chosen processes?

1141. Did the delivered product meet the specified requirements and goals of the Loyalty and Rewards project?

1142. Did you do things well?

1143. What could be done to improve the process?

1144. How dependent is the Loyalty and Rewards project on other Loyalty and Rewards projects or work efforts?

1145. How will staff learn how to use the deliverables?

1146. What level of risk does the proposed budget represent to the Loyalty and Rewards project?

5.1 Procurement Audit: Loyalty and Rewards

1147. Did the organization identify the full contract value and include options and provisions for renewals?

1148. Are review meetings organized during contract execution and do they meet demand?

1149. Where an electronic auction was used to bid, were all required specifications given equally to tenderers?

1150. How do you avoid delays at any stage/ stages of the procurement process?

1151. Does the strategy ensure that appropriate controls are in place to ensure propriety and regularity in delivery?

1152. Were the tender documents comprehensive, transparent and free from restrictions or conditions which would discriminate against certain suppliers?

1153. Are existing suppliers that have a special right to be consulted being contacted?

1154. Is it clear which procurement procedure the organization has opted for?

1155. Has an upper limit of cost been fixed?

1156. If an order is divided among several vendors, is the explanation for that procedure documented?

1157. Does the organization have an overall strategy and/or policy on public procurement, providing guidance for procuring entities?

1158. Where funding is being arranged by borrowings, do these have the necessary approval and legal authority?

1159. Are vendor price lists regularly updated?

1160. Are bank accounts reconciled by an individual independent of the disbursement responsibilities?

1161. Are goods generally ordered and received in time to be used in the programs for which they were ordered?

1162. Have late payment interests been rewarded and could they have been avoided?

1163. Does the organization maintain a current file of vendors and vendor catalogues?

1164. Is the procurement process well organized?

1165. Is there no evidence that the expert has influenced the decisions taken by the public authority in his/her interest or in the interest of a specific contractor?

1166. Does the procurement function/unit have the ability to apply public procurement principles and to prepare tender and contract documents?

5.2 Contract Close-Out: Loyalty and Rewards

1167. What happens to the recipient of services?

1168. What is Capture Management?

1169. How is the contracting office notified of the automatic contract close-out?

1170. How does it work?

1171. A change in circumstances?

1172. Parties: Who is Involved?

1173. Parties: Authorized?

1174. Was the contract sufficiently clear so as not to result in numerous disputes and misunderstandings?

1175. Was the contract type appropriate?

1176. Are the signers the authorized officials?

1177. Has each contract been audited to verify acceptance and delivery?

1178. Have all acceptance criteria been met prior to final payment to contractors?

1179. Have all contracts been closed?

1180. Why Outsource?

1181. Have all contracts been completed?

1182. How/When Used ?

1183. Was the contract complete without requiring numerous changes and revisions?

1184. A change in knowledge?

1185. Have all contract records been included in the Loyalty and Rewards project archives?

1186. A change in attitude or behavior?

5.3 Project or Phase Close-Out: Loyalty and Rewards

1187. Is there a clear cause and effect between the activity and the lesson learned?

1188. If you were the Loyalty and Rewards project sponsor, how would you determine which Loyalty and Rewards project team(s) and/or individuals deserve recognition?

1189. Was the user/client satisfied with the end product?

1190. What went well?

1191. Who is Responsible for Award Close-out?

1192. What is a Risk Management Process?

1193. Does the lesson educate others to improve performance?

1194. What Security Considerations needed to be addressed during the Procurement Life Cycle?

1195. What are the informational communication needs for each stakeholder?

1196. What are the marketing communication needs for each stakeholder?

1197. Which changes might a stakeholder be required

to make as a result of the Loyalty and Rewards project?

1198. Does the lesson describe a function that would be done differently the next time?

1199. What could have been improved?

1200. Have business partners been involved extensively, and what data was required for them?

1201. What advantages do the an individual interview have over a group meeting, and vice-versa?

1202. What hierarchical authority does the stakeholder have in the organization?

1203. Is the lesson based on actual Loyalty and Rewards project experience rather than on independent research?

1204. What information did each stakeholder need to contribute to the Loyalty and Rewards projects success?

5.4 Lessons Learned: Loyalty and Rewards

1205. How efficient were Loyalty and Rewards project team meetings conducted?

1206. Overall, how effective were the efforts to prepare you and your organization for the impact of the product/service of the Loyalty and Rewards project?

1207. If issue escalation was required, how effectively were issues resolved?

1208. How effectively were issues managed on the Loyalty and Rewards project?

1209. How closely did deliverables match what was defined within the Loyalty and Rewards project Scope?

1210. What would you like to see better documented about how to use existing processes on this type of Loyalty and Rewards project?

1211. What was the geopolitical history during the origin of the organization and at the time of task input?

1212. How useful was your testing?

1213. How effective were the techniques used to prepare you and your organization for the impact of the changes brought about by the product or service produced by the Loyalty and Rewards project?

1214. What on the Loyalty and Rewards project worked well and was effective in the delivery of the product?

1215. How effectively and timely was the organizational change impact identified and planned for?

1216. How much of your time was spent on other than this Loyalty and Rewards project?

1217. Is there any way in which you think our development process hampered this Loyalty and Rewards project?

1218. How effective was each Loyalty and Rewards project Team member in fulfilling his/her role?

1219. How well did the scope of the Loyalty and Rewards project match what was defined in the Loyalty and Rewards project Proposal?

1220. Was the Loyalty and Rewards project manager sufficiently experienced, skilled, trained, supported?

1221. What things surprised you on the Loyalty and Rewards project that were not in the plan?

1222. How effective were the communications materials in providing and orienting team members about the details of the Loyalty and Rewards project?

1223. Whom to share Lessons Learned Information

with?

1224. What things mattered the most on this Loyalty and Rewards project?

Index

managers 2, 101, 103, 112, 185, 220
manages 112, 223
managing 2, 8, 101, 106, 175, 210
mandate 105
mandatory 195
manner 163-164, 182, 194, 224
mantle 83
mapped 28
market 21, 143, 219
marketer 7
marketing 87, 232
markets 20
material 127
materials 1, 235
matrices 119
Matrix 3-5, 107, 119, 163, 177, 189
matter 33, 35, 41
mattered 236
matters 197
maximise 221
maximize 209
maximizing 85
maximum 103
meaning 204
meaningful 42, 91, 128
measurable 28-29
measure 2, 11, 19-20, 30, 32, 34, 37-40, 42-45, 48, 50, 55-56, 58-59, 63-64, 69, 73-74, 76, 154, 160, 214
measured 17, 34-35, 37-38, 41-44, 65, 68, 75, 160, 163
measures 35, 37-38, 40, 42-44, 46, 48, 53, 61, 68, 75, 158-159, 215, 221
measuring 74, 128
mechanical 1
mechanized 130
medium 187, 218
meeting 30, 70, 150, 155, 162, 166, 185-186, 191, 202, 204-205, 233
meetings 26-27, 29, 121, 197, 228, 234
megatrends 96
member 5, 24, 97, 141, 169, 191, 208, 215, 235
members 23, 25, 27, 29, 33, 113, 122, 130-131, 147, 150, 165, 167, 169-170, 176, 181-182, 190, 203-210, 214-215, 220, 235
membership 207-208

reported   184, 219
reporting   72, 115, 128, 157, 186, 216, 221
reports 42, 106, 111-112, 115, 121, 130
repository   131, 167, 181
represent   65, 155, 196, 227
reproduced   1
reputation   86
request   5, 50-51, 155, 167, 184, 193-196
requested   1, 64, 183, 193, 195
requests   193
require 39, 71, 73, 105, 140, 148, 171, 214
required   20, 28-29, 32, 56, 75, 102, 114, 123, 132-135, 143,
146, 152, 161, 170, 174-175, 187-188, 190, 228, 232-234
requiring   106, 231
research   21, 89, 136, 199, 204, 233
resemble   183
reserve 128
reserved   1
reserves   131
reside 131
resistance   188
resolution   47, 122, 170
resolved   151, 182, 234
Resource   3-4, 8, 109, 114, 130, 140-141, 143, 163, 167, 182,
191
resources   2, 8, 18, 26, 30, 37, 56, 65, 71, 74-75, 88, 92, 94,
105, 107, 114, 132, 134-135, 139, 141-143, 146, 149, 151, 153, 185,
188, 202, 213, 215
respect   1
respond   110
responded   12
response   17, 21, 71-72, 75, 187, 222
responses   173, 184
responsive   153
result   48, 60, 65, 154-155, 195, 206, 214, 230, 233
resulted   76
resulting   47, 111
results 8, 24, 28, 43, 47, 55, 58-59, 63-65, 68, 70, 102, 109-110,
114, 131, 153, 158-159, 161, 176, 208, 213
Retain 77
retained   168
retrospect   98
return   43, 60, 85, 157, 162